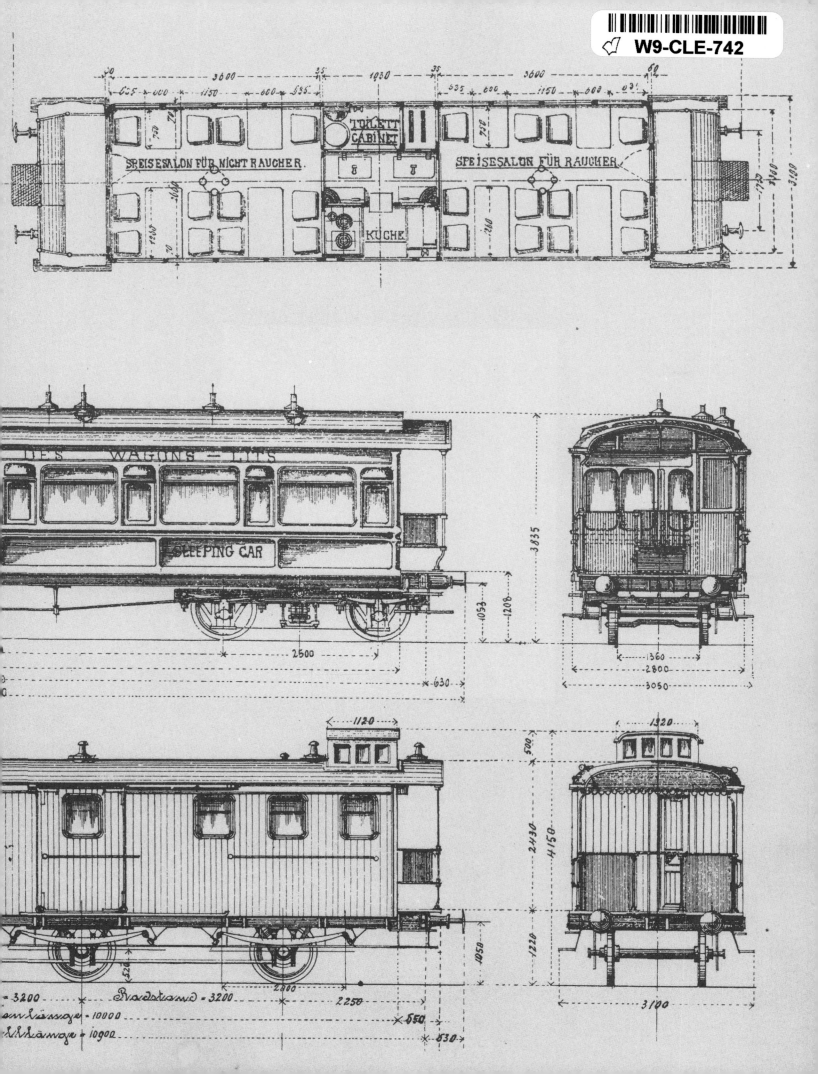

SPEISESALON FÜR NICHT RAUCHER.

TOILETT CABINET

KÜCHE

SPEISESALON FÜR RAUCHER

DES WAGONS - LITS

SLEEPING CAR

3835

2500

1053

1208

630

1360

2800

3050

1120

500

2430

4150

3200

Radstand = 3200

2800

2250

550

630

1220

1050

3100

THE
ORIENT EXPRESS

THE
ORIENT EXPRESS

THE HISTORY OF THE ORIENT EXPRESS SERVICE FROM 1883 TO 1950

Anthony Burton

CHARTWELL
BOOKS, INC.

Published by
CHARTWELL BOOKS, INC.
A Division of **BOOK SALES, INC.**
114 Northfield Avenue
Edison, New Jersey 08837

ISBN: 0-7858-1352-7

Editorial and design by
Amber Books Ltd
Bradley's Close
74–77 White Lion Street
London N1 9PF

Project Editor: Jill Fornary
Design: Zoë Mellors
Picture Research: Lisa Wren

Printed in Italy

Frontispiece:
The Anatolian Express steaming through Turkey in 1925.

Contents

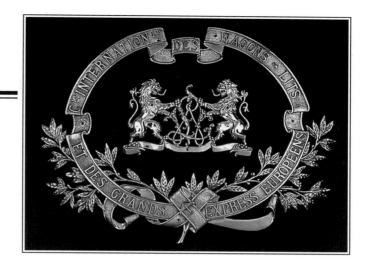

The very first run of the Orient Express in October 1883, with the French Est 500 class locomotive heading a train consisting of a mail fourgon, two sleeping cars, a dining car and a baggage fourgon.

CHAPTER ONE

Beginnings

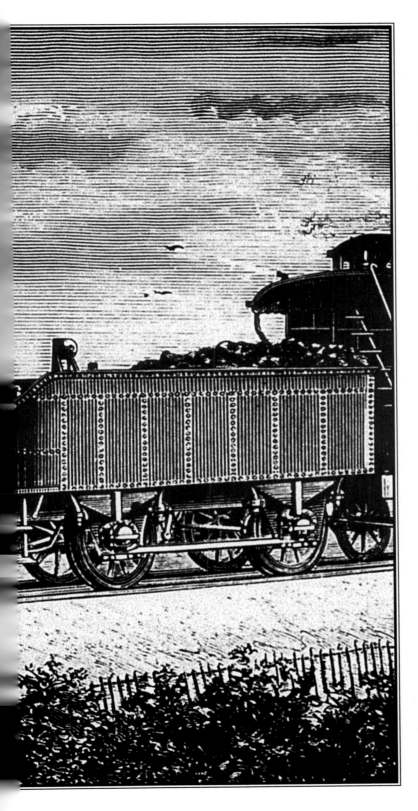

The nineteenth century was the great age of the railways. It began modestly when a tiny locomotive hauled a train of wagons down a rickety track in South Wales in 1804, yet already by the middle of the century steam railways had reached all around the world. But it had all been done piecemeal. It was not just that individual countries planned their routes with little thought to what their neighbours were doing; the private companies who built and ran the lines within most of those countries were more interested in competition than co-operation. The larger vision was often lost among squabbling factions. Yet it was possible to think big. In America they had to do just that, if the grand dream of a rail link from the east coast to the west was to be realised.

On 10 May 1869, at Promontory Point, Utah, the Central Pacific Railway, which had forced a route through the Sierras, met the Union Pacific that had raced across the plains. The world's first transcontinental railway was complete. But could such unity ever be achieved in a politically complex Europe, with its independent and often mutually suspicious countries? One man believed it could be done, and acted on his beliefs. His name was Georges Nagelmackers.

Nagelmackers was born in Liège, Belgium, in 1845. This was a young country, which had only gained independence from the Netherlands in 1832, when Leopold of Saxe-Coburg became King Leopold I of Belgium. New as it was, it already had a diverse and flourishing industrial base, and no time was wasted

before the government began promoting railways. In 1835, the first train steamed out to unite Brussels with Malines (Mechelen). Railways cost a great deal of money, and prominent among the financiers who backed the development was the powerful banking family of the Nagelmackers. They were wealthy, well connected, and Georges' father enjoyed a close, friendly relationship with the king. It was just the sort of business in which a son of the family could be certain of financial success, a secure future and social prestige. But of all the bank's activities, it was the railways that fascinated young Georges, which is perhaps not too surprising. Throughout his boyhood, the system was still being developed, and the Nagelmackers were at the heart of it. But acting as banker to a great railway company did not somehow have the glamour of running it oneself. And in Georges' case, he saw no reason to limit his activities to just one country, for the family had business and social connections that spread across Europe. Brought up to think in terms of international high finance, and with a passion for railways, he began to dream of a train that would take its passengers right across the continent to the borders of Asia.

GO WEST, YOUNG MAN

As a young man, his passions were not entirely restricted to railways. He fell in love, wooed – and was rejected. It is not certain whether he travelled to heal a wounded heart or whether his parents were intent on ending an inappropriate liaison. At least he could pursue his other love, and what better place for a young man with a dream of a transcontinental railway to go than the only place that had one? In 1869, he arrived in America, land of optimism, a country on the move. This was a rowdy, thrusting nation of startling contrasts: while the bankers discussed finance in New York, men such as 'Wild Bill' Hickok were establishing law by the six-gun in the cattle towns that had sprung up along the new railways. The States of America may have been United, but the communities the railways served were as varied as anything Europe could offer, while the physical difficulties faced by the railway builders were every bit as daunting. It was a huge encouragement to Nagelmackers to see what could be achieved. And the American railway system had already provided answers to some of the technical problems of long-distance travel.

The earliest rail journeys were generally short, and the idea of luxury extended little beyond padding the seats of the first-class carriages and putting glass in the windows (the latter was not deemed necessary in second class). The third-class carriages were

LEFT *In this formal portrait, Georges Nagelmackers, the founder of Wagons-Lits, looks very much a member of one of the great banking families of Europe. He was also a visionary who was to fulfil his dream of a railway that would join Europe to Asia.*

little better than cattle trucks, and had no windows to glaze. The ride provided by even the best coaches was rough; four-wheeled coaches being the norm. A typical first-class coach of the 1840s had three compartments, each holding six passengers, and looking rather like three stagecoaches shunted together, but with only four wheels between them. By the 1860s, more comfortable six-wheelers had started to appear, which were nevertheless still quite primitive. As there were no interconnecting corridors, refreshment cars were unknown. The same was true of toilets: trains waited in stations for passengers to attend to the call of nature. Sleepers were rare, but collapsible beds, rather like hospital stretchers of the time, could be installed in some coaches by special arrangement. There were some luxury coaches, most famously provided for the use of royalty: Queen Victoria's Great Western saloon of 1842 even had a semaphore on the roof to send messages to the driver asking him to go slower if need be. Such was the world that Nagelmackers knew; what he found in America was very different.

American tracks were laid with light rails, often set in very sharp curves. A European six-wheeler could hardly have negotiated such a system, and as early as the 1840s Americans were building carriages carried on two bogies, each with four wheels, so that the front and rear wheels could swivel independently. This gave a far smoother ride than the fixed-axle coaches of Europe, an important factor when considering journey times measured in days rather than hours. Such a journey would need a small hotel on wheels, with toilet facilities, refreshments and beds. This was what Nagelmackers had in mind, and already an American had shown the way forward.

Nagelmackers could hardly have timed his arrival in America more opportunely, for here he met a man with similar ideas to his own, and who had already made a breakthrough in improving rail travel. The very first sleeping car had appeared on the Cumberland Valley Railway in 1836, and in one of those early, crude cars, so the story goes, a young man and his bride set off on their honeymoon in the 1850s. The man was George Mortimer Pullman, and the experience made him all too aware of the shortcomings of the existing system. He tried to interest the railroad companies in his notion of a better class of car, which would double as a parlour car by day and a sleeping car by night. He bought a day coach from the Chicago & Alton Railway, and converted it into his first sleeper. The public, it seems, was not quite ready for luxury travel, and the conductor had great difficulty persuading the passengers that they should take their boots off when going to bed. Eventually, Pullman and his associates had a modest fleet of twelve cars, but they were not a great success, and were in any case commandeered when the Civil War began in 1861. The war was not all bad news for Pullman, however, for he made a considerable amount of money as a trader, supplying goods to Colorado gold miners – enough

for him to buy the materials for a far superior carriage, a very substantial vehicle of timber construction on an iron frame. It ran on two four-wheeled bogies, fitted with springs and rubber shock absorbers for a steady ride. Most impressive, however, was the interior. Gone were the old separate compartments, and in their place was a parlour car with comfortable chairs, which at night could be converted into beds, with an upper bunk pulled down above them. These ran the length of the compartment. Everything was luxurious, from the thick pile carpet to the panelled walls, brass lamp fittings, embroidered seat covers and, less romantically but more importantly, the toilets. He named it *Pioneer*.

TOP *On a visit to America in 1867, Nagelmackers travelled in Pullman cars of this type, and was impressed and inspired by them. By day the carriage is a respectable parlour on wheels.*

ABOVE *At night, with the Pullman's bunks made up, the passengers were secluded only by flowing curtains – a feature which the Belgian considered shockingly improper.*

RIGHT *A bearded Leopold II of Belgium disembarks at Beaulieu, France, in 1907. The first subscriber to Nagelmackers' new company, he was a regular passenger, and not just when on official business: his mistress, Cléo de Merode, had a house in Beaulieu.*

It was not just a very luxurious coach, it was also big and heavy, too big in fact for the railway companies, who declined to use it. Pullman desperately needed some way to get his car into service, and his opportunity arrived with the assassination of President Abraham Lincoln in 1865. It was decided that the body should be taken from Washington to Lincoln's birthplace in Illinois. Pullman offered *Pioneer* for the journey, and the offer was accepted. If bridges were too narrow or parapets too high, then they had to be altered, for nothing must impede the solemn progress of the funeral train, which attracted huge attention. More publicity soon followed. General Grant, the hero of the

Union Army, was also going home, but in his case in triumph, and once again *Pioneer* did the honours. Now everyone knew of the luxury coach, and orders began to come in from the railways that had previously dismissed the whole idea. Among the distinguished visitors granted a ride was Georges Nagelmackers. He not only inspected the coach in detail, but quizzed Pullman on his plans for establishing long-distance routes. Though it is not known whether he saw an actual example, he must also have been aware of Pullman's other innovation – the 'hotel car'. This doubled as sleeping car and diner. The upper bunks folded away during the day, there were tables between the seats and a

kitchen at one end of the car. The American's plans included establishing a Pullman service in Europe, and he might have been a good deal less free with his information had he known that the young Belgian was about to emerge as his main competitor.

Nagelmackers spent a year in America and his time was not wasted. He saw that a luxury train was a practical possibility, with through trains running over the boundaries set by competing companies, just as he hoped to run trains across international boundaries. He learned a lot about improving construction and new ways of designing coach interiors, but he had strong views on which ideas could be best adapted for the European market. He did not think that a coach layout that suited democratic Americans going about their business would be equally suitable for European aristocrats travelling with

whole train. The answer was the compressed-air brake, invented by George Westinghouse in 1869. Operated by a pump on the locomotive, it worked through pipes laid in every coach, and connected together by flexible hoses. The system was still being developed during Nagelmackers' visit, but it was already clear that the fundamental problem of braking heavy trains had been solved. There were no technical problems that could not be overcome, and so the way was open for Nagelmackers to introduce a new generation of luxury trains to Europe. All he needed to do was raise the capital, design and build the coaches, and persuade a phalanx of railway companies in different countries to accept a foreign, or virtually stateless, train onto their tracks.

PLAYING THE ROYAL TRUMP

Back in Liège, the enthusiastic Georges consulted his father about financing the scheme. It was here that the royal connection proved invaluable. Leopold II, who was now on the throne, was an enthusiast for the British pattern of building a wealthy nation based on empire and industry. He is now best remembered for his infamous role in turning the Congo not so much into an imperial possession as a personal fiefdom run for profit. Leopold was forever in need of money to maintain the lifestyle becoming a monarch. The Nagelmackers played on this need. They were offering a vision of a Europe-wide network of trains, based on Belgian enterprise, that would be the envy of the world. And there would be profits. The king was not asked to invest cash – only to give his name and royal blessing. So Nagelmackers et Cie was created, with the name of Leopold II heading the list of subscribers. In April 1870, a promotional brochure was produced: *Projet d'installation de wagons-lits sur les chemins de fer du continent* – a project for establishing sleeping cars on continental railways. It was the first time anyone had used the phrase 'wagons-lits' in print.

The first steps were designing and building the coaches. The start was tentative. Nagelmackers had returned enthused by new ideas: a quite new type of carriage, new wheel arrangements and an improved braking system. All were within the capabilities of European manufacturers, but there was a danger in trying to do too much too quickly. The new company had to work within an existing framework. Its cars had to be adaptable, so that they could be coupled on to trains run by different companies all over the continent. In addition, Nagelmackers had no wish to frighten people off by building cars to a radically different

servants, and obsessed with protocol. One thing was clear: the railway world was moving towards ever bigger and heavier coaches, and this created new problems. The first trains had brakes on the engine and on a special van at the back of the train, hence the name 'brake van'. As power increased, the hand brake gave way to the steam brake on the engine, but what was now needed was a system that would operate right through the

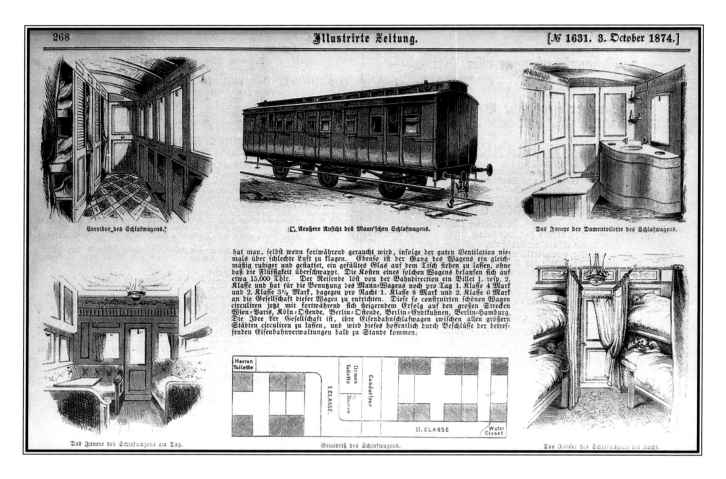

design, unknown and untested in Europe. There were no bogies and no air brakes, and externally the first cars had nothing new to offer. The differences were all on the inside. American trains were not only undivided by class, there were no allowances made for the differences between the sexes either, so that young ladies had to go to bed with no more than a curtain to protect them from the eyes of men passing to and fro in the car. In Nagelmackers' cars there were three separate compartments, each holding four comfortable chairs that were folded down at night to make into beds. Five vehicles were ordered from a firm in Vienna, a choice dictated as much by diplomacy as by manufacturing merit. The right to cross Austria was essential to the company's long-term plans, and a train of locally built coaches could prove more acceptable than a Belgian one. Later, production was mainly centred on the Rathgeber Works in Munich.

The first planned route was from Paris to Berlin. It is surprising that a family as well connected as the Nagelmackers should have seemed so blithely unaware of the growing tensions between France and Prussia. Early in July 1870, the new carriages were ready to roll – and the Franco–Prussian War promptly began. There was much hurried consultation before Georges Nagelmackers came up with a new route, from Ostend to the Adriatic port of Brindisi in Southern Italy, bypassing the battlefields. It was complicated to set up, involving as it did

ABOVE *A set of illustrations showing the exterior and interior of the Mann Boudoir Car in 1874. Compartments are made up for day and night use, with the upper bunks hinged up against the wall for daytime travel. There was a single toilet compartment at one end of the coach.*

contracts with France, Austria, Switzerland and Italy, but well worth it. The British proved good customers, keen to avoid the long voyage through the Straits of Gibraltar. Now with P & O liners calling at Brindisi, they could shorten the journeys to Africa and Asia. Nagelmackers also got a mail contract, and the coaches were regularly booked by diplomatic staff. Five more cars were ordered, and the weekly service soon became twice weekly. Everything was going well until the war ended. The French had been at work on the Mont Cenis tunnel through the Alps since 1857, and now they could proceed with greater speed. When it opened in 1871, it offered a far shorter route to Italy than Nagelmackers', and it was strictly reserved for French trains. He lost his British contracts, and the Brindisi service withered.

CUSTER'S COLONEL TO THE RESCUE
Nagelmackers responded to the crisis with bravado. Out went Nagelmackers et Cie, and in came La Compagnie Internationale des Wagons-Lits. The name at first proved

grander than the operations. There were no grand trains made up of Wagons-Lits cars, simply the odd coach attached to a regular service train, which was available to anyone prepared to pay a supplement. Very few thought it worth the expense, particularly for short journeys. At this stage the returns on what had been a considerable investment were not so much low as insignificant. Just as the situation was looking desperate, Nagelmackers received an invitation from an American businessman, Colonel William Mann, who wanted to discuss a possible partnership. Mann was a genuine colonel, having fought in the Civil War under Custer, but there was little else genuine about him. His previous career had included selling shares in an oil company with no oil, and a job as tax collector for Alabama, to which he applied a 'one dollar for the government, one dollar for me' principle. His first railway involvement had been the promotion of a bogus company. He did then move on to a genuine enterprise, building luxury coaches called 'Boudoir Cars'. Like Pullman, he had an eye for publicity, and he provided a special car for the most famous beauty of the day, Lillie Langtry. In America, however, he was faced with the well-established Pullman empire, hence his decision to try his luck in Europe, with

an approach to Nagelmackers. In his desperate plight, the Belgian was not overly thorough about checking references. All too quickly convinced by the wealthy 'railway tycoon', he settled for a role as junior partner and The Mann Boudoir Sleeping Car Company was established. The first cars were ordered from an English factory.

Mann applied the tactic that had worked so well in America, this time supplying a coach for the Prince of Wales to attend a royal wedding in St Petersburg. In a sense, the publicity was too successful, for it alerted Pullman to the presence of a rival in Europe. It was time to mount a challenge. In a straight battle, the might of Pullman would have easily outmatched the puny Mann enterprise; but Mann did not favour a clean fight. He mounted a campaign hinting at immorality in the open Pullman coaches, something quite impossible in the safety of a closed Boudoir coach. This was a trifle rich, as Mann was in the process of building a car for Leopold II in which he could entertain his mistress, Cléo de Merode. The carriage was to become known to

BELOW *A staff card of 1874, bearing William Mann's signature. This pass allowed the named person to use the Boudoir Car without paying the usual supplement.*

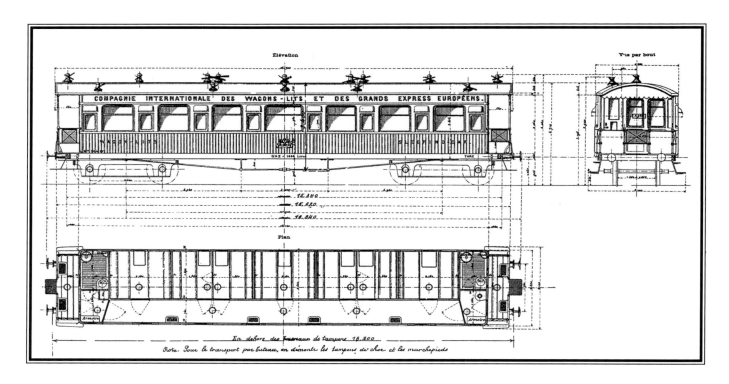

ABOVE By 1880, notable improvements had been made in the rolling stock, of which the most important was the mounting of the cars on two four-wheeled bogies. This new technology gave passengers a more comfortable ride.

BELOW A sectional model of sleeping car No. 60 built by Wagons-Lits for the Belgian section of the 1878 International Exhibition. It differs from the first sleeping cars in having the main frame and springs set inside the wheels.

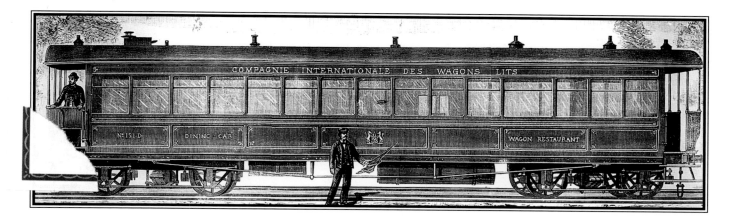

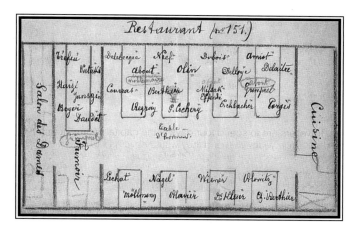

ABOVE *Dining car No. 151 D, which was used in the inaugural run of the Orient Express. The use of two four-wheeled bogies instead of six wheels on three axles, as on earlier carriages, produced such a smooth ride that it was said wine glasses could be filled to the brim with no fear of spillage.*

RIGHT *The seating plan for the very first journey of the Orient Express. Nagelmackers is seated at one of the tables for two, while the three journalists on board were well separated – About and de Blowitz in the main compartment, Boyer in the smoking room at the end of the car.*

satirists of the time as the 'Cléopold'. While Nagelmackers plodded across Europe obtaining orders, Mann stayed in London doing very little apart from spending his share of the profits as, typically, he showed little concern for any long-term interests. It was soon clear to Nagelmackers that not only was Mann doing nothing to help the business, but his unsavoury reputation was positively harmful. The American was seen as no better than a confidence trickster, which appalled Nagelmackers. Completely honest and respectable himself, he realised his association with Mann was bringing his own name, and that of the family banking institution, into disrepute. Mann and his backers were bought out, his name was expunged from the business and the Compagnie Internationale des Wagons-Lits was reborn in 1876.

Nagelmackers now began the long process of negotiating running rights for Wagons-Lits over various lines. Some were highly prestigious, linking Paris to other capitals such as Rome and Berlin, and also to Calais for the British trade. In 1882, he introduced his first dining car on a trial run from Marseilles to Nice. At its centre was a tiny kitchen with pantry, wine cellar, and coal-fired stove. The choice of coal for the stove was wholly practical, since that was the one fuel the train was always going to carry. On either side of the kitchen were the two saloons, each with twelve places, providing a general saloon suitable for ladies and a separate smoking saloon for gentlemen. The

sections were linked by corridor. Everything was done in high style, from the leather upholstery to the elaborately painted ceilings. There was a gas tank big enough to ensure the coach could be lit for twenty-six hours. It was a huge success, and Nagelmackers finally felt ready to achieve his dream.

He had personally followed tortuous routes around Europe to find the best possible way to link Paris to Constantinople (Istanbul) and had negotiated rights for a train made up entirely of Wagons-Lits coaches to cover the journey. Running via Strasbourg, Salzburg, Munich, Vienna, Budapest and Bucharest, it was to be the first-ever Orient Express. At this time the company assumed its full, magniloquent name: Compagnie Internationale des Wagons-Lits et des Grands Express Européens. Several trial runs were made, before selected dignitaries were invited to assemble at what was then Paris's Gare de Strasbourg, now the Gare de l'Est, on 4 October 1883. Among them were two well-known writers, Edmond About, popular novelist and respected journalist, and Henri Opper de Blowitz, Paris correspondent for the *Times*. They both wrote full and enthusiastic accounts of the journey.

As the passengers gathered in the late afternoon, they may have felt a touch disappointed to see a standard Wagons-Lits six-wheeler standing by the platform. This was a touch of pure Nagelmackers theatre, intended to heighten the contrast with

what was to come. For when the real train appeared, they saw a splendid rake of new coaches, resplendent in a gleaming, royal-blue livery. At their head was a 2-4-0 Class 500 locomotive of 1870 from the Est company. Although based on a design that had originated many years previously at the London and North Western Railways works at Crewe, this was a fine engine, with its two pairs of 5ft (1.5 metre) diameter driving wheels, inclined cylinders and high shiny dome. And Nagelmackers had incorporated the new American technology, for the engine was equipped to pump air to the Westinghouse brakes on the new cars. Behind the tender was the first of two *fourgon*s, or baggage, cars. This one contained the mail, an important source of revenue for Wagons-Lits, since the passengers were all travelling free and

would be enjoying lavish hospitality. A second *fourgon* held the passengers' luggage and, very importantly, the wine reserves.

Placed between the *fourgon*s were the coaches: two sleeping-car saloons and a dining car. These were brand new bogie cars, very similar to Pullman's, and they proved a revelation to the male passengers, who for the first time on any European train could shave without fear of cutting their own throats. Each *wagon-lit* held twenty passengers, who wallowed in the luxury of leather-embossed chairs in compartments panelled in teak and mahogany enlivened by exotic marquetry. And as night fell, the chairs were made into beds, complete with silk sheets. Each car had two toilets in the care of a discreet, uniformed attendant, who nipped in after each passenger to clean and polish so that everything was

ABOVE *This richly appointed early restaurant car boasts velveteen window blinds and chairs covered in Moroccan leather. At one end of the carriage was a smoking room for the men; at the other, a boudoir for the ladies.*

LEFT *The honour of hauling the very first Orient Express train out of Paris fell to a powerful 500 class locomotive such as this, built at Epernay in 1870 for the French Eastern Railway Company, L'Est.*

pristine for the next visitor. But what really impressed the guests was the dining car. Here, French design at its most overblown was on display. Gas chandeliers cast light on a scene of baroque opulence – scarcely a surface escaped from scrolls, curlicues, swags of flowers in marquetry and gilt. All very fine, but before the Parisians would pass comment on the dining car, it had to pass the test of the gourmets. And pass it did. Georges Boyer, special correspondent of *Le Figaro*, was moved to describe the Burgundian chef as a genius. He was particularly impressed by the way the menu was varied to reflect the taste of the country through which they were passing, complemented by the wines of the region.

The staff were as splendid as the carriages. In overall charge was the *chef de train*, though needless to say his rule did not extend as far as the kitchen. Under him were the *conducteurs* (conductors), one per compartment, all decked out in peaked caps, smart, gold-braided uniforms and highly polished boots. For the occasion they wore arm bands, with the monogram OE making its first appearance. The waiters wore white gloves while serving at table, a true vote of confidence in the steadiness of the new rolling stock. There were lesser officials who helped with baggage, in a hierarchy of employees that ended with the lowly kitchen boy.

STEADY SHE GOES

The starting point was the Gare de l'Est, which, with no fewer than thirty platforms, was splendid testament to the abundant optimism of the early years of railway design. As the train gathered speed through the Paris suburbs, the passengers assembled for the first of many spectacular meals. Even when a speed of 50 mph (80 kph) was reached, the tables were as steady as if they stood in a boulevard restaurant. Opper de Blowitz, a man to whom such things were of great importance, reported with pleasure that he was served red wine, white wine and champagne in brimming glasses without a drop being spilled. As the guests finally retired, they also noted that they could enjoy the luxury of both hot and cold water, a rarity on trains in those days.

At 5.30 a.m., the express arrived at Strasbourg, where the station master was on hand to show off the wonders of the electric lights, the first to be installed at any European station. Sadly, few passengers had recovered from the mighty dinner,

and all that About, semi-official chronicler of the run, could write was that someone had told him 'they looked well'. The train now headed north up the Rhine valley, then east again to the Danube, which, About caustically noted, was not blue at all, but *schmutzig* – the 'Grimy Danube'.

On the approach to Munich, there was an unfortunate delay involving a hot axle-box in the dining car. The train crawled into Munich to collect a replacement car that was on standby – a wise precaution on Nagelmackers' part. At midnight, some thirty hours after leaving Paris, they pulled into Vienna, where the all-male party was leavened by the arrival of two ladies, Madame von Scala, wife of an Austrian minister, and her sister, Mlle Pohl – an event that interested M. About much more than the electric lights at Strasbourg. So the train travelled on, passing the 1000-mile mark, to arrive at the twin cities of Buda and Pest. All was tranquil as the

train rolled through Hungary, past vineyards and fields of pumpkins, but the peace was broken as it steamed into Szeged. Here, they were met by an ebullient band of Tzigane musicians who, About declared, 'had the devil in their fingertips'. It broke the monotony of the Hungarian plain, and the diversion did not end there, for as the train pulled out, the musicians leaped on board, and the sedate carriage rocked to dancing in the aisles. The episode ended with a performance of 'La Marseillaise', with the Burgundian chef leading the chorus in a voice as big as his menus.

At Bucharest, the company had organised a special treat, an excursion to Sinaia in the heart of the Transylvanian Alps. Here, King Carol of Rumania had built the Peles Palace as his summer retreat, a building more romantically medieval than any actual medieval building had ever been. The party greeted the news that the king had decided to grant an audience at the palace with

LEFT *An 1883 sleeping car interior; one compartment is made up with four beds, while the other is arranged for day use, with the upper bunks folded down to form the backs of the seats.*

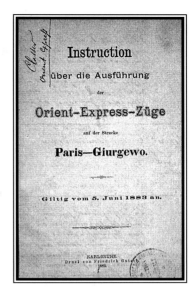

RIGHT *A staff instruction manual, dated 5 June 1883, for the running of the train between Paris and the Romanian town of Giurgiu, bordering Bulgaria. As this was an international operation, the text is in French and German.*

BOTTOM RIGHT *Henry Opper de Blowitz's account of the first run of the Orient Express appeared in book form as* Une Course à Constantinople *(An Excursion to Constantinople), with this handsome cover embossed in gold.*

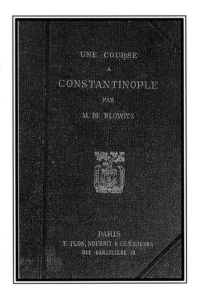

something less than enthusiasm. Gentlemen accustomed to court protocol were not keen to appear in front of royalty in their everyday attire, but they were reassured to learn that the king understood this and would not stand on ceremony. Worse was to come. It appeared that the king, thinking the party would enjoy a mountain walk, had not sent any transport. The weather turned bad, and they arrived wet and begrimed only to be confronted with the king in full ceremonial uniform. To this embarrassment was added the miserable thought that they would soon be slithering down the track they had just scrambled up.

They now looked forward to spending the rest of the journey cosseted in the luxury of the Orient Express. Nagelmackers, however, had neglected to mention that there was, as yet, no through rail link to Constantinople. The train stopped at the Danube, which formed the frontier between Rumania and Bulgaria, with not a bridge in sight. Instead, they had to take a dubious-looking ferry to the opposite bank, to join a train that would take them onwards, but not in the style they had come to enjoy. The prospect ahead offered no comfort. The track was wretched, the land was crawling with bandits who often robbed stations and, even worse, lifted lengths of track to cause derailments. The train crawled along, still not heading for Constantinople itself, but only for the Black Sea port of Varna. It arrived without incident, and the passengers embarked on a steamer for the last leg of the journey. Enduring the choppy waters and the wallowings of the aged steamship, they at last reached their ultimate destination. After an orgy of sightseeing, they left to retrace their steps, returning to Paris on 13th October. After eleven days of travel, they drew into the Gare de l'Est, precisely on time. It had been a bold venture, and a resounding success.

The year is 1906 and the lady preparing to board dining car No. 1651 D appears to be very grand for not only has the conductor come out to greet her, but also the chef de brigade *in full livery with knee breeches. In fact, this was an early publicity photograph.*

CHAPTER TWO

The Early Years

The inaugural run had been an undoubted success, but there was no denying that the latter part of the journey had come as a considerable anti-climax. Consequently, Nagelmackers set about finding a new route to Constantinople. The most obvious, direct way was to turn south at Budapest for Belgrade, and from there take a direct line, down through Serbia and Bosnia through what was then known as Turkey-in-Europe, to Constantinople. The trouble was that while some of the necessary rail links existed on the ground, others were still at the planning stage, and the rest had not even been considered. Nagelmackers was faced with delicate political negotiations on the one hand and formidable engineering challenges on the other.

The line had to pass through Serbia and Bulgaria, whose governments had to be convinced that they wanted an expensive railway system at all. They had to be persuaded of the long-term advantages of, and the profits that would accrue from, having the main rail route linking western Europe and Asia pass through their territory. Having argued the merits of this, Nagelmackers still had to convince them that they should grant his own company, Wagons-Lits, running rights across their borders. The agreements were reached and rights granted, but with some irksome conditions that reflected worries about the terrain and the climate on the part of authorities, who still viewed railways as a dangerous novelty. A weight limit was set for the train of 100 tons in good weather. In heavy snow, or if the temperature fell below

HORAIRE DU GRAND EXPRESS D'ORIENT

Paris-Vienne-Constantinople

Station		Arrivée.	Départ.	Arrêts.
PARIS....	London, départ 10 mat.		7.30 soir.	
La Ferté-s.-Jouarre	Calais, arrivée. 1.40	8.34 soir.	8.39 »	5
Epernay...	Calais, départ. 2.16	9.42 »	9.47 »	5
Châlons-sur-Marne	Châlons, arriv. 9.35	10.18 »	10.26 »	8
Bar-le-Duc	Mardi et Vendredi	11.41 »	11.45 »	4
Toul		12.51 mat.	12.54 mat.	3
Nancy		1.27 »	1.35 »	8
Lunéville		2.11 »	2.12 »	1
Igney-Avricourt		2.40 »	2.41 »	8
Deutsch-Avricourt		2.44 »	*Heure allemande.* 3.12 »	1
Sarrebourg		3.36 »	3.37 »	1
Saverne		4.09 »		
Strasbourg		5.02 »	5.07 »	5
Kehl		5.29 »		
Appenweier		5.42 »	5.47 »	5
Oos (Baden-Baden)		6.22 »	6.26 »	4
Carlsruhe		7 »	7.05 »	5
Durlach		7.13 »	7.14 »	1
Pforzheim		7.48 »	7.50 »	2
Mühlacker		8.08 »	*Heure de Stuttgard.* 8.16 »	5
Stuttgart		9.18 »	9.23 »	5
Geislingen		10.44 »		
Ulm		11.30 »	*Heure de Munich.* 11.45 »	5
Augsbourg		1.24 soir.	1.27 soir.	3
München		2.35 »	2.40 »	5
Simbach		5 »	*Heure de Prague.* 5.16 »	5
Wels		7.04 »	7.10 »	6
Amstetten		8.45 »	8.49 »	4
Saint-Pölten		9.59 »	10.03 »	4
WIEN (West Bahnhof)		11.15 »	11.25 »	10
WIEN (Staatsbahnhof)			12.01 mat.	
Marchegg	hre de Prague heure de Pest	1.00 mat.	1.04 »	4
»		1.18 »	1.22 »	4
Pressburg		1.54 »	1.57 »	3
Wartberg		2.27 »	2.31 »	4
Neuhäusel		3.47 »	3.51 »	4
Gross-Nana		4.38 »	4.42 »	4
Budapest		6.09 »	6.17 »	8
Czegred		7.56 »	8 » »	4
Felegyháza		9.13 »	9.17 »	4
Szegedin		10.31 »	10.36 »	5
Mokrin		11.29 »	11.33 »	4
Hatzfeld		12.14 soir.	12.17 soir.	3
Temesvar		1.06 »	1.14 »	8
Lugos		2.39 »	2.43 »	4
Karansebes		3.36 »	3.40 »	4
Porta-Orientalis		4.50 »	4.54 »	4
Herkulesbad		5.49 »	5.51 »	2
Orsowa		6.16 »	6.21 »	5
Verciorova		6.30 »	*Heure de Bucharest.* 7.45 »	37
Turn-Severin		8.07 »	8 09 »	2
Craiova		10.50 »	11 » »	10
Slatina		12.24 mat	12.28 mat	4
Pitesti		2.18 »	2.23 »	5
Bukarest		4.45 »	5.15 »	30
Giurgevo (Smârda)		6.45 »		
Roustschouk			9.31 mat	
Tchernavoda		10.09 mat	10.14 »	5
Rasgrad		11.50 »	11.51 »	1
Ischiklar		12.31 soir	12.32 soir	1
Scheytandjik		1.12 »	1.30 »	18
Schoumla-Road		2.16 »	2.21 »	5
Pravady		3.09 »	3.10 »	1
Gubodjie		4.02 »	4.03 »	1
VARNA		4.31 »		
» (Lloyd Austro-Hongrois)			6.25 »	
CONSTANTINOPLE	Samedi et Mardi.	6.00 mat		

Constantinople-Vienne-Paris

Station		Arrivée.	Départ.	Arrêts.
CONSTANTINOPLE......	Jeudi et Dimanche		12.30 soir.	
VARNA......			5.00 mat.	
Gubodjie		5.29 »	5.30 »	1
Pravadi		6.22 »	6.27 »	5
Schoumla-Road		7.15 »	7.20 »	5
Scheytandjik		8.18 »	8.30 »	12
Ischiklar		9.23 »	9.24 »	1
Rasgrad		9.58 »	9.59 »	15
Tchernavoda		10.20 »	11.25 »	5
Roustschouk		12.00 soir.		
Giurgevo (Smârda)			*Heure de Bucharest.* 1.30 soir.	
Bukarest		3 »	3.15 »	15
Pitesti		5.29 »	5.34 »	5
Slatina		7.14 »	7.18 »	4
Craiova		8.35 »	8.43 »	8
Turn-Severin		11.21 »	11.23 »	2
Verciorova		11.43 »	*Heure de Pest.* 11.25 »	10
Orsowa		11.34 »	11.44 »	10
Herkules-Bad		12.09 mat.	12.11 mat.	2
Porta-Orientalis		1.12 »	1.16 »	4
Karansebes		2.13 »	2.17 »	4
Lugos		2.58 »	3.02 »	4
Temesvar		4.15 »	4.23 »	8
Hatzfeld				
Mokrin		5.38 »	5.43 »	5
Szegedin		6.28 »	6.33 »	5
Felegyháza		7.35 »	7.39 »	4
Czegled		8.37 »	8.41 »	4
Budapest		10.02 »	10.08 »	6
Gross-Nana		11.25 »	11.28 »	3
Kurth		11.50 »	11.54 »	4
Neuhäusel		12.14 soir.	12.17 soir.	3
Wartberg		1.20 »	1.23 »	3
Pressburg		1.49 »	1.50 »	1
Marchegg	heure de Pest hre de Prague	2.12 »	2.15 »	3
WIEN (Staatsbahnhof)		1.54 »	1.57 »	3
»		2.47 »		
(Westbahnhof)		3.20 »	3.25 »	5
St-Pölten		4.40 »	4.44 »	4
Amstetten		5.54 »	5.58 »	4
Wels		7.33 »	7.39 »	6
Simbach		*Heure de Munich.* 9.30 »	9.24 »	5
München		11.44 »	11.49 »	5
Augsburg		12.57 mat.	1. » mat	3
Ulm		*Heure de Stuttgart.* 2.39 »	2.34 »	5
Geislingen				
Stuttgart		4.35 »	4.40 »	5
Mühlacker		*Heure de Carlsruhe.* 5.44 »	5.45 »	4
Pforzheim		6.01 »	6.02 »	1
Durlach		6.37 »	6.38 »	1
Carlsruhe		6.46 »	6.52 »	6
Oos (Baden-Baden)		7.30 »	7.35 »	8
Appenweier		*Heure de Strasbourg.* 8.10 »	8.15 »	8
Kehl		8.30 »		
Strasbourg		8.48 »	8.53 »	5
Saverne		9.44 »		
Sarrebourg		10.19 »	10.20 »	1
Deutsch-Avricourt		*Heure française.* 10.43 »	10.21 »	
Igney-Avricourt		10.24 »	10.47 »	23
Lunéville		11.10 »	11.11 »	1
Nancy		11.47 »	11.55 »	8
Toul		12.30 soir	12.33 soir	3
Bar-le-Duc		1.40 »	1.44 »	4
Châlons-sur-Marne		2.53 »	3.01 »	8
Epernay		3.35 »	3.40 »	5
La Ferté-sous-Jouarre		4.48 »	4.52 »	4
PARIS		6. » »		

NOTA. — *Consulter l'Indicateur des Wagons-Lits, en cas de changement dans l'horaire du Grand Express d'Orient.*

-4°C (25°F), then at least one sleeping car would have to be dropped, and, if things got really bad, then anyone wanting to continue the journey would have to find whatever space they could in the dining car. The conditions were agreed, but never featured very prominently in the company's brochures.

In 1885, tunnelling commenced to overcome the greatest physical obstacle – the mountains between Dragoman and Sofia. Meanwhile, the Orient Express had to make the best it could of the new southern route. The line was open from Budapest to Belgrade and for a further 200 miles (321 km) to Nisch, now Nis. The Company did their very best to persuade potential customers of the delights of the journey, and in particular of the pleasures of Nisch itself. Beyond Budapest, the writer of the brochure informed his readers – in obvious desperation – that they could look out of the window and see a lot of cows and large flocks of sheep – hardly a prospect to stir the blood. Nisch, not exactly a metropolitan centre, with its rough, cobbled streets and mud-brick houses, was described as 'the second capital of Serbia'. One attraction was the Hotel de l'Europe, which offered a room for four francs, a good meal with unlimited wine for three francs; and, if the wine was not to one's liking, there was an excellent beer from the local brewery. The main appeal, however, for those who had travelled this far, was the striking scenery, for Nisch was surrounded by mountains rising to a height of around 6000 feet (2000 metres). It was a pleasant place to linger and, truth to tell, lingering there was probably a better option than carrying on with the journey.

A STATE OF DILAPIDATION

Where the railway came to an end, the journey continued by diligence, a small but well-sprung stagecoach – and passengers had good cause to be grateful for the springing, for the next stage proved to be a bumpy ride. The anonymous writer did his best, however, to make this part of the journey, up through a mountain pass to Pirot, seem like a jolly scenic excursion. After a very early morning start, there was a steady climb through often beautiful scenery, which, the publicist assured everyone, would more than compensate for leaving the comfort and luxury of the train behind. There was a grisly monument to be glimpsed along the way: a 'Tower of Skulls', relic of a bloody siege in the Turkish–Serbian war, which ended in 1830. At Bela Pelanka, there was a halt of two or three hours allowing refreshment for the passengers and a rest for the horses. Even the enthusiastic publicist could find little to say about this hill village, other than it boasted another Hotel de l'Europe. The last leg of the day down to Pirot must have looked encouragingly short as the crow flies, but the carriage road zigzagged endlessly on the long descent, so that although Bela Pelanka to Pirot is no more than 6 miles (10 km) in a direct line, the journey took a full five hours. It was a very weary, creaky-jointed set of passengers who left the coach for the dubious pleasures of Pirot. The best that could be said of this place was that it was 'picturesque'. A less kindly visitor spoke of 'an indescribable state of dilapidation'. At least the Hotel Roi de Serbie was cheap, with a mere three francs covering room and board.

LEFT *In 1883, the train was known as the Grand Express d'Orient, its name changing to the Orient Express eight years later. This timetable shows departures from Paris on Tuesdays and Fridays, returning from Constantinople on Thursdays and Sundays.*

RIGHT *This announcement, dating from 15 November 1886, warns would-be passengers that places are very limited. Clients are advised to book in advance at the company's agency at the Place de l'Opéra in Paris, and are reminded to buy first-class tickets.*

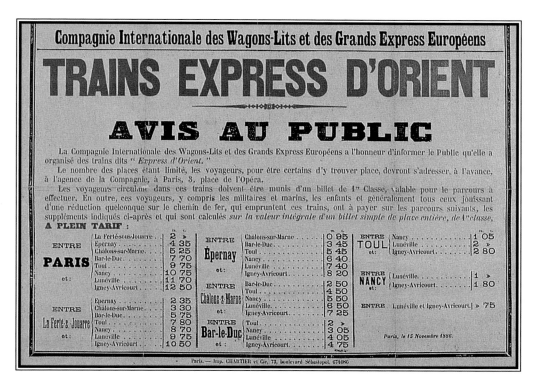

ABOVE A poster of 1905, showing a variety of compartment interiors and concentrating very much on the luxury on offer, from the dining car with its panoramic views to the richly carpeted salon. Private toilet facilities may not have been as romantic, but were still sufficiently novel to earn their place in the overall picture.

LEFT A major improvement to the service in the 1880s came with the opening up of a rail link through Bulgaria, and to celebrate the event the Orient Express staff posed for this photograph at an unnamed Bulgarian station. The gentleman in the handsome, double-breasted uniform is the chef de train.

Another day of coach travel lay ahead, through spectacular mountain gorges, which offered some compensation for the filthy resting places along the way. The last stage, from Sofia onwards, was the most demanding of all, with rough tracks and extreme gradients that almost brought the horses to their knees. At last, after a three-day journey, the weary travellers reached the railhead at Tatar-Bazardjik (Pazardzhik). As a place, it had as little to commend it as the squalid villages passed en route, but at least here the cramped diligence was left behind for the comforts of a railway carriage. The accommodation, though not on a par with that offered by the luxury *wagons-lits*, must have seemed heaven after what had gone before. And the company made the proud boast that they would now be whirling along at the dizzy speed of 26 mph (42 kph). The Sea of Marmara finally came into view, and, at six in the evening, after twelve hours on the rails, the train finally pulled into Sirkedji (now Sikerci) Station in Constantinople, splendidly sited between the quays of the Golden Horn and the great dome of Saint Sofia.

There was no getting away from the fact that, regardless of the official purple prose, this was a long and wearisome journey. It is not surprising to find that few passengers booked for the through trip: it is simply astonishing that any booked at all. Everyone was aware of the shortcomings, not least the railway engineers building the new lines. Nevertheless, they did their work well, blasting and hacking their way through the mountains with remarkable speed. Early in 1889, the work was complete. On 1 June of that year, a train, composed entirely of Wagons-Lits rolling stock, left the Gare de l'Est, and the passengers were able to enjoy the facilities of the dining car and the comforts of the saloons until, sixty-seven hours and thirty-five minutes after leaving Paris, they arrived at Constantinople. The Orient Express really was a true express at last.

Improvements soon got under way and, by 1894, two hours had been shaved off the schedule. That same year, the Fetesi bridge was completed across the Danube, opening up a through route from Bucharest to the Romanian port of Constanta on the Black Sea. Where Varna had been an apology for a harbour, with ships forced to anchor offshore to be serviced by a flotilla of dubious small craft, Constanta was a genuine port, where passengers could embark directly from the quays. The passage by steamer down to Constantinople usually took rather more than twenty-four hours, but the service used modern ships with high standards of comfort. So now, Wagons-Lits, after struggling for five years to provide a service that met its own high standards, was in a position to offer two alternative Orient Express routes. Other alternatives were to appear over the years.

At last, all seemed well; the difficult years were over, and the Orient Express could look forward to a prosperous and peaceful future. Then, on 3 May 1891, the unthinkable happened: the Orient Express was robbed. The train was on its final leg, just 60 miles (96 km) from Constantinople, near the town of Cherkes Keui (Cerkesköy) in Eastern Thrace. It consisted of a locomotive and tender, a baggage car, two local coaches and, at the rear, three Wagons-Lits cars. The driver suddenly realised that the track up ahead had been sabotaged, but had no time to halt the engine. He and the fireman leaped for their lives as the locomotive plunged down an embankment, dragging the coaches behind it. The link to the Wagons-Lits cars snapped under the impact, leaving them upright on the track, while the local coaches tumbled down.

At once a band of men appeared, looking for all the world like stage bandits, bristling with guns and knives. But this was no pretence. The Wagons-Lits staff were taken off the train and trussed up at the trackside. Then, the passengers, some nursing cuts and bruises from flying luggage, were herded into the corridors. Armed men smashed open everything they could find, in the hunt for valuables. The leader, Anasthatos, an immense black-bearded Greek, informed them in a bewildering mixture of French, German and Greek that they were not to worry. His men were not really bandits at all, but valiant

RIGHT *In 1898 the Orient Express had become so famous that it was made the subject of a Montmartre cabaret. It is ironic that the service designed by Nagelmackers to avoid the immodesty of the American Pullman cars should become the inspiration for a saucy nightclub revue.*

LEFT This brochure of 1897 bears a sun and moon motif – most apt for a train that runs both day and night. By this time the service was already being offered on a daily basis.

RIGHT Wagons-Lits was always happy to accommodate visiting dignitaries. Theodore Roosevelt was given use of the presidential car in 1900.

freedom fighters – which did not stop them from removing everything of value. The passengers were, however, reassured that no one would be harmed. When one of them resisted, he was shot in the arm, at which the infuriated leader laid his own man low with a single punch. With an air of gallantry, he then returned wedding rings and other items of merely sentimental value. So far, the experience might have been worth it just to have a tale to dine out on, but the ordeal was not yet over.

The passengers were lined up and hostages selected, including the unhappy driver, who was still recovering from his leap from a careering locomotive, and five German businessmen. As the party disappeared, the passengers released the Wagons-Lits staff, who set about tidying up the train and making the distressed passengers as comfortable as possible. At daylight, one of the hostages, a chef at the British Embassy in Pera, was released with a message that the ransom was £8000 or 200,000 francs to be paid in gold, otherwise the remaining hostages would be shot. The message was reinforced when a German banker was escorted to the police, bearing the same message. Nine days after the incident, the ransom was paid and the hostages were released, each with five gold sovereigns, a last quixotic gesture from Anasthatos. The Greek was never captured, nor were any of the valuables ever recovered.

OUTRAGE ABROAD

An investigation into the robbery of an international train and the abduction of prominent citizens was not to be left to the local police. As the news of the incident spread, there was international outrage. Kaiser Wilhelm II threatened to send troops across the border to capture the brigands, which was tantamount to an act of war. The Sultan in Constantinople was outraged at the loss of international prestige for the empire. Officials were sacked, troops moved into the region in force and draconian measures taken to end banditry. Inevitably, Nagelmackers was criticised for sending trains, packed with some of the wealthiest passengers in Europe, through such a

notoriously unstable and dangerous region. From that point of view, the opening of the alternative route to Constanta could not have come at a better time. If his clients were concerned about kidnapping – and worse – Nagelmackers could direct them to this far safer route. On the other hand, the whole affair brought huge press coverage and, at least, by the end of it there were very few people who did not know of the Orient Express. The general air of Ruritanian melodrama that surrounded the whole event made it seem almost romantic – if not to the unfortunates who were actually involved. The Orient Express was no longer just another train; it had acquired a reputation for mystery, intrigue and danger – something that it was never really to lose.

This was reinforced by the presence of some very exotic passengers, and few were more exotic than Sir Basil Zaharoff. The name was the one he used later in life, but he was a man of

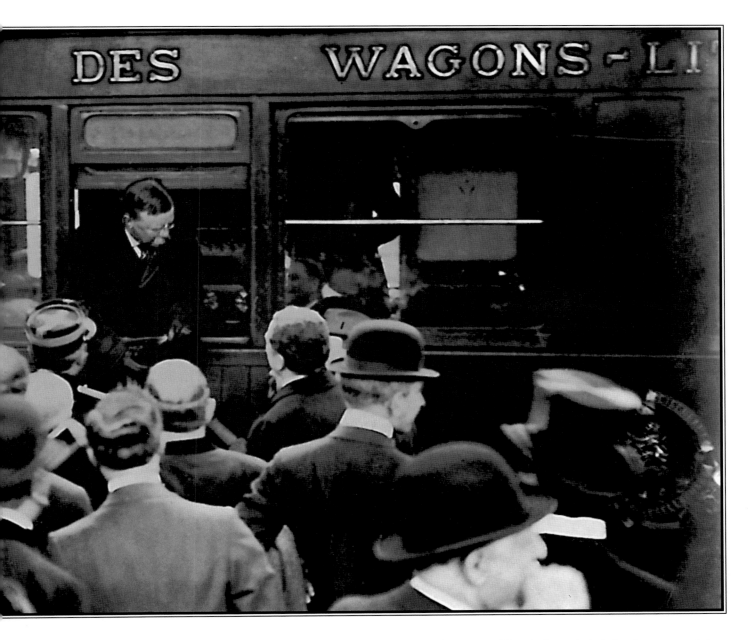

so mysterious a past that no one was entirely sure about his origins. Certainly nothing in his background indicated that one day he would receive honours ranging from the Grand Cross of the Légion d'Honneur in France to the Order of the Bath in Britain. His early years were spent as a 'guide' in Constantinople, a familiar euphemism for pimp. As a young man, he travelled widely in eastern Europe, prepared to trade in anything that showed a profit. Chance brought him into contact with the armaments industry and the Swede Torsten Nordenfelt, who had designed a submarine that no one seemed to want to buy. Zaharoff, with his knowledge of Balkan intrigues, persuaded Nordenfelt to let him act as salesman on commission. He went first to Greece, where he convinced government officials that the possession of such a vessel would give them an immediate advantage over their Turkish rivals

across the Aegean. The deal concluded, he then proceeded to remove that same advantage by selling submarines to Turkey. He became, almost overnight, a man of wealth and power, adept at playing on the nervous rivalries of the Balkan states. As his business interests stretched right across Europe, and were particularly strong in the East, the Orient Express became, in effect, his commuter train. Whenever he travelled, he was automatically given the same compartment, No. 7. His taste for good living extended to a penchant for red-headed girls, who were generally slipped on board and into No. 7 at Vienna, and returned to Austria in equal style and comfort once Zaharoff had left the train. He would always have been a remarkable figure in the annals of the Orient Express, one of those men around whom all kinds of stories are woven. But his place was assured during a journey in January 1886.

Among the other passengers were the Duke of Marchena and his eighteen-year-old bride, Maria Berente, daughter of Count Fermin de Miguero y Azcarte. Niceties of personality are seldom considered to be of great importance in dynastic marriages, and no one had seen fit to mention to the girl that her new husband suffered from severe mental disturbance. As the train approached Salzburg, Zaharoff heard screams in the corridor and opened his compartment door to see what was happening. The young woman collapsed inside, her nightdress ripped and blood dripping from a deep scratch on her throat. She blurted out in terror that her husband was trying to kill her, a claim that needed no further verification when the man himself appeared brandishing a knife. Zaharoff's bodyguard overpowered the Duke, who was led away, in a state of collapse, to his

compartment. The Duchess stayed with Zaharoff. At the end of this memorable journey, the Duke was quietly removed to a private nursing home and the young lady became Zaharoff's mistress. The couple had three daughters, and, when the Duke died, they were finally able to marry in Paris in September 1924. The honeymoon, inevitably, included a journey from Paris in compartment seven on the Orient Express.

Another regular traveller on the Orient Express was involved in an equally dramatic incident. Calouste Gulbenkian was born to a wealthy Armenian family, living in Asian Turkey. He was destined in later life to make a huge fortune in oil, but in 1896 his only concern was to save his own life and that of his young wife and child. Over the years, the Armenian minority had been subjected, with the rest of the non-Turkish population, to an

increasingly violent campaign against them. The more extremist Armenians resorted to violence in retaliation. This was the excuse the Sultan needed. He made it quite plain that no mercy should be shown, and dropped strong hints that all Armenians could be regarded as potential, if not actual, terrorists. The mobs took to the streets in an orgy of murder, while the authorities looked on. Gulbenkian and his wife dressed in their oldest, poorest clothes, she with a bundle on her head, he with a rolled carpet tucked under his arm. To all appearances, they were Turkish carpet-sellers going about their business, but her bundle contained gold coins and jewels; and wrapped up inside the carpet was their baby son, Nubar. Where other Armenians were desperately trying to make their escape by boat, and seldom succeeding, the Gulbenkians made their way to the Orient Express. It is a tribute to the almost legendary composure of the Wagons-Lits staff that they accepted an apparently impoverished carpet-seller and his wife into a first-class compartment without demur. Over the years, Gulbenkian was to be a regular user of the train, and it was said that, at every stopping place en route, a house or room had been purchased and a girl installed, with nothing to do but wait for the multi-millionaire to put in an appearance.

Wealthy patrons could book as much first-class accommodation as they felt they required, but for heads of state something much grander was in order. In 1887, a whole set of

LEFT A dining car of 1890, gas-lit, with good insulation, a heavily carpeted floor and abundant stocks of wine, all making for a highly congenial atmosphere. Here, the table napkins are folded exactly as they were at the inaugural dinner, as described by About.

BELOW The collapse of a bridge in Turkey in 1899 sent carriages plummeting into the river, but miraculously there was no recorded loss of life. On the whole, the Orient Express enjoyed a very good safety record.

salon, sleeping and restaurant car was built specifically for the use by the president of France. Each coach was emblazoned with the letters PR, for Président de la République, but could equally well have stood for excellent Public Relations. The first to make use of them was President Carnot, though not with very good fortune: while stepping down from the special train at Lyon in 1894, he was assassinated by an anarchist. This did not deter later presidents. But, luxurious as the coaches were, they were not considered quite grand enough for the visit of Czar Nicholas II, the Czarina and an assortment of Russian ministers and court officials. Wagons-Lits was given just six weeks to convert seven coaches into wonders of extravagant opulence. The original PR1 became a bedroom with double bed, twin bathrooms resplendent in gold plate, and separate compartments for the royal attendants. The customary tables of the dining car were removed and replaced by one immense banqueting table. All seven coaches were completely transformed, and the Wagons-Lits lilies were well and truly gilded. It was an immense effort to complete the work on time, but Nagelmackers was rewarded with the right to run his special coaches over the newly opened Trans-Siberian Railway.

A NEEDLESS FATALITY

Having royalty travelling on the Orient Express gave it a special cachet, but it could also create its own peculiar problems. King Ferdinand of Bulgaria not only had his own salon-car, but he developed a passion for steam locomotives. He considered it a royal prerogative to be allowed onto the footplate to take over the controls in his own kingdom. No one was prepared to argue, but there were some unfortunate incidents. On one occasion he woke up in the middle of the night, and decided he would like to take over at the regulator. But how was he to communicate with the driver? His answer was to pull on the emergency brake handle of his salon-car. The train juddered to a stop, the brakes on the rest of the train seized, and it was to be several hours before it could move on. The company was not amused, and requested that in future he should use more orthodox means of joining the driver in his cab. Ferdinand, who had backed the German side in the 1914–18 war, was forced to abdicate in 1918. But his son Boris, an even more avid rail enthusiast than his father, became king. One of Boris's exploits had a tragic end. The Orient Express was running late, so Boris decided to do

LEFT The Orient Express dining car at its most extravagant, with a wealth of elaborate detailing from the ornate brass fittings to the swagged drapery. Here, travellers enjoyed the finest cuisine on offer anywhere in the world, with every effort being made to cater for even the most extravagant and eccentric of tastes.

something about it. With the regulator wide open, he kept demanding more steam. The pressure gauge needle reached, and passed, the danger mark, forcing the professional driver to do what he could to blow off some of the excess steam. Meanwhile, the king was urging the fireman to heap more coals on what was already a small inferno in the firebox. The unfortunate man opened the doors and the fire blew back, engulfing him in flames. He fell, clothing ablaze, from the engine. The king simply ignored the incident, and the train sped on. The death of a fireman was, it seems, a small matter compared with the heroic efforts of the King of Bulgaria to bring the Orient Express in on time. How much money had to be paid to the unhappy man's family to keep the matter quiet is not recorded.

Famous passengers are only a part of the Orient Express story. The train was a success because it provided a much-needed service, and provided it efficiently and with style. The success of the operation depended on many factors. First, there was the quality of the product on offer. Nagelmackers was constantly updating and improving the rolling stock. By the end of the century, he was replacing the old *wagons-lits* with a new generation of coaches, linked by flexible 'concertina' connections. The new standards had eighteen berths per car, with wash-basins and commodes. New restaurant cars were also built, with improved suspension. To make sure that everything was kept in first-rate condition, the company established its own maintenance workshops all round Europe. The new cars not only looked better, they were better in every way. When the Express was derailed on the Bucharest route in 1899, the results could have been catastrophic, but in fact the coaches and their passengers survived the accident remarkably well. Wagons-Lits was so pleased that it put out a brochure explaining that if, heaven forbid, an accident should happen, the passengers could be reassured by the knowledge that they were travelling in the best-constructed and safest carriages to be found on any railway in the world.

Some problems, however, were outside the control of Wagons-Lits. In 1892, a cholera epidemic swept through Turkey, and all trains were quarantined for a time. This was followed by a severe winter when temperatures fell as low as -24°C (-11°F), and in places the line was blocked by 3 feet (1 metre) of snow. At this time, the dining cars were run as a concession, with a catering company providing kitchen staff and waiters. With few trains actually running, and few passengers wanting to risk either disease or freezing to death, the catering staff had no income and were forced to find other jobs. One effect of this was to convince Wagons-Lits that it was, after all, better served when everyone was under its own control. The only good news was that the mail service was still proving profitable, though even here there were problems. Two diplomatic couriers took great exception to the Turkish authorities' demand that the official mail should be sprayed with disinfectant. Not unreasonably, the Turks insisted that public health came before protocol, and foreign embassies had to make do with somewhat aromatic correspondence.

LUXURY, SPLENDOUR AND DISCRETION

Those who travelled on the Orient Express expected, and got, luxury accommodation, but just as importantly they also got splendid, and, if need be, very discreet service. Just as Wagons-Lits preferred to service its own rolling stock, so too it preferred to be responsible for training its own staff to exacting standards. With the best rolling stock and the best staff, all that was needed for a thoroughly successful operation was equally good organisation. The Orient Express was quite unlike most other railway systems in that it owned no track or engines, and ran through many different states and nations, over an immensely varied terrain, coping with mountains, plains and extremes of climate. Different countries had their own characteristics, with different loading gauges and special safety regulations, so that the smooth running of the train required constant adjustments and a clear knowledge of local requirements. This need was reflected in the organisation of Wagons-Lits. Although it was a Belgian company, the headquarters, the *Direction Générale*, were in Paris, with the French government represented on the board. Below this were the individual *direction*s, one for each country through which the trains ran. Nagelmackers knew that running a railway successfully depended on solving practical and technical problems, so each of the national offices was headed by an engineer, rather than a professional administrator. It was a system that usually worked very well indeed. There was, however, never any sense of complacency, and the company was always on the look-out for ways to improve the service – and so attract still more passengers. One thing was quite obvious: why should the provision of luxury accommodation end just because the train had reached its final destination? In 1894, an offshoot of the main company was formed, the Compagnie Internationale des Grands Hôtels, and soon it was offering visitors to Constantinople a choice. Right in the heart of the city, with magnificent views, was the splendid Pera Palace, but when the stifling heat began to rise from the crowded streets, the visitors could stay instead in the cooler, but no less grand, Therapia Palace on the far side of the Bosphorus. Travellers could now be

RIGHT Dining was a relatively formal affair in the years just before World War I. In this photograph of 1912, the waiters, resplendent in their knee breeches, could easily be serving in a first-class hotel.

assured of the same high standards from the time the train was first boarded in Paris, through their stay in the Turkish capital, until they again stepped out onto the platform of the Gare de l'Est.

There was one group of passengers whom Nagelmackers had always been keen to attract to his splendid train, but, for them, the difficult part was getting to Paris in the first place. They were the British, inconveniently separated from the continental system by the English Channel. They had already proved that they appreciated the type of superior accommodation offered by Wagons-Lits by the enthusiasm they had shown for its great rival, Pullmans. These had obtained a foothold in the British market as early as 1873, when Pullman himself agreed a fifteen-year contract with the Midland Railway to supply and operate rolling stock. If the British were to be wooed by a continental company, then it would make sense to have a British representative on the board. The man invited to join Wagons-Lits was Davison Dalziel, later Lord Dalziel of Wooler. He was thirty-nine years old, but had already proved himself a successful entrepreneur. Much of his early business life had been spent in America, and on his return to England he had set up the Dalziel News Agency, which was eventually to run the London *Evening Standard*. He also founded the General Motor-Cab Company, which

introduced motor cabs to London streets in place of the old horse-drawn hackneys. Most importantly of all, he had recently purchased the British Pullman Car Company. This was just the sort of connection Wagons-Lits was looking for. He joined them in 1893, and was on good terms with Nagelmackers from the first, a relationship that was cemented when his daughter Elizabeth married Nagelmackers' son René.

Dalziel was soon involved in negotiations for a cross-channel link. In 1905, plans were drawn up between the South Eastern & Chatham Railway and the Chemin de Fer du Nord for a train ferry from Dover. Special vehicles were to be built by Wagons-Lits that were to include a *fourgon-buffet*, a variation of what the French called a *fourgon-fumoir*, a baggage car that had a compartment where gentlemen could relax over cigars on the uninterrupted journey from London to Paris. The idea was to create a London club on wheels. However, the bill to authorise the running of a train ferry was rejected by the British parliament. The idea was not forgotten, merely shelved for a number of years. In spite of this failure, Dalziel's influence continued to grow under Nagelmackers' benevolent gaze.

Nagelmackers could look with considerable pride on what he had achieved with Wagons-Lits. He fixed on 1873, the year he had joined forces with Mann, as the starting date, and in 1898

ABOVE Wagons-Lits conductors posed together at Ostend in 1898 for a special photograph to mark the company's 25th anniversary.

LEFT The firm's principal booking agency in Paris was this splendid building with its fine wrought-iron balconies, photographed circa 1900.

RIGHT The special menu of 4 January 1898 for Wagons-Lits' anniversary dinner.

BELOW When passengers arrived in Constantinople, they were offered accommodation at the resplendent Pera Palace. Guests were ushered into the ornate lift by a uniformed attendant.

ABOVE This sumptuous dining car of 1899, featuring velvet curtains and leather seats, was divided into two sections, each with two tables for four diners, and two for couples.

RIGHT Wagons-Lits car No. 1000 was displayed as a prototype at the Liège Exhibition of 1905. It was built with the wheels on six axles, an idea that was not developed beyond this example.

he prepared to celebrate the twenty-fifth anniversary. In his home town of Liège, he took over the only building large and grand enough for the occasion, the Music Conservatory. There he staged a banquet for some two hundred guests. The twelve-course dinner started with oysters and concluded with 'Glaces Wagons-Lits', elaborate confections, shaped into the form of carriages and piled with ice cream. After fighting their way through the mountain of food, helped on their way by abundant supplies of fine wines, many guests no doubt dozed through the long series of speeches and eulogies. Liège was again the centre of attention when Nagelmackers was one of the organisers of an International Exhibition. Among the prize exhibits were the finest examples of Wagons-Lits workmanship. Restaurant Car No. 999 was much praised, and visitors particularly admired the elaborately painted Italian ceilings. It was joined by the new No. 1000 sleeping car. The next big occasion to be marked was the Silver Jubilee of the Orient Express in 1908, but Nagelmackers did not live to see it. Shortly after visiting the Liège exhibition, he died of a heart attack on 10 July 1905. Wagons-Lits was about to enter a new age under new management, with Dalziel now in charge as its new president.

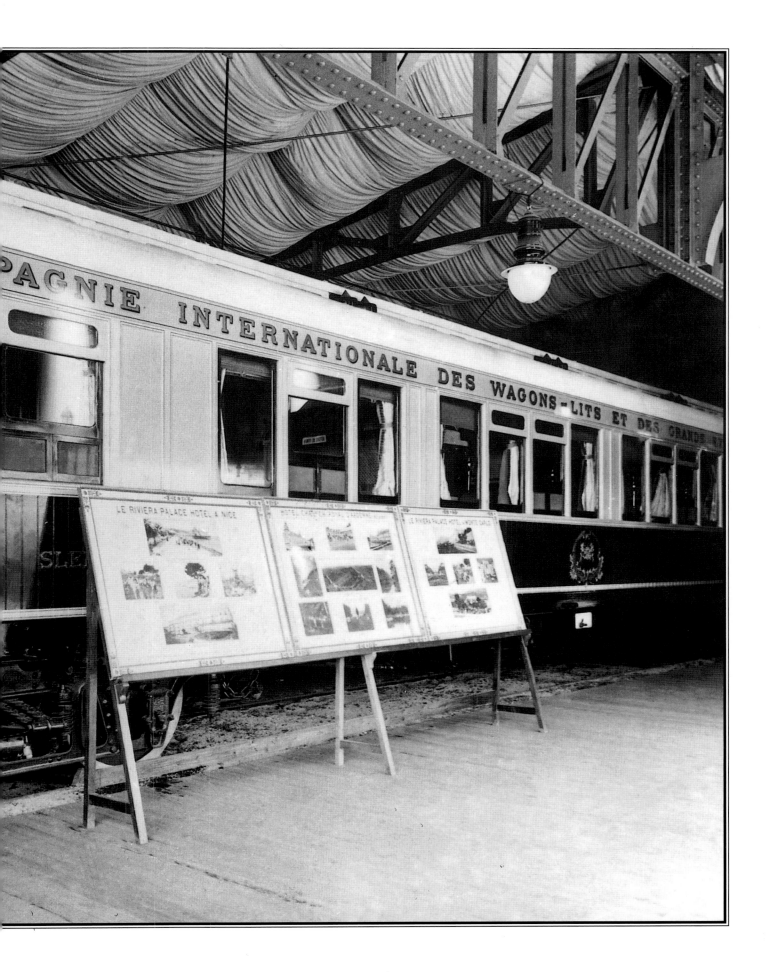

Before the opening of the night ferry British passengers for the Orient Express had to disembark at Calais, while porters carried their luggage from the ship to the waiting train. This was the scene at Calais Maritime in the 1930s.

The Golden Years

The early railway builders were men of vision, and it took both vision and supreme self-confidence to think of constructing a line through the heart of the Alps, linking France, Switzerland and Italy. They looked at a route that had been in use for centuries, the Simplon Pass. The Romans had come this way, and had built a military road. By the thirteenth century, a hospice had been established at the top of the pass to provide a resting place on what was still little better than a track. Napoleon marched his troops over the pass to the battlefield of Marengo, and, after his victory when he was crowned King of Italy, he built another military road that writhed and twisted over the mountains. In October 1805, the first stagecoach used the same road.

A photograph taken a century later shows a coach on the road, quite a small vehicle that required a team of five horses to pull it. Opening the Napoleonic road had been considered something of a civil engineering triumph, yet in 1857, just ten years after Switzerland had seen the opening of its first modest line from Zurich to Baden, plans were being promoted for a tunnel under the Simplon Pass. They came to nothing, as did the other thirty or so plans that, as well offering variations on the tunnel, proposed rack railways and cable railways to run over, rather than through, the Alps. Real progress began in 1889, when the Swiss government invited Italy to send delegates to a conference in Berne to discuss a rail link. Final agreement was only reached in 1895, but the technical problems that had

to be addressed were immense. At a length of almost 12 miles (20 km), this would be the longest railway tunnel in the world, and it was to be bored through mountains whose peaks would rear up some 4250 feet (1300 metres) above the tracks. Not surprisingly, the plans were subjected to the most careful scrutiny, for the engineers' estimates for the work came out at a colossal 69,500,000 francs. To give the figures a context, the reader might recall that four francs at that time was the price paid by Orient Express passengers for a room at the best hotel in Nisch. A permanent office was established at Berne, with officials from Switzerland and France, and in 1898 work got under way.

The plans called for not one but two tunnnels. The second, a smaller service tunnel, was built with the idea that eventually it would be enlarged to take tracks when the volume of traffic demanded it. The construction work was entirely dependent on water power. Aqueducts were built at either end to provide a head of water for hydraulic drills, air compressors and for the very necessary job of cooling the work sites as the men probed ever deeper under the mountains – at the Swiss end, the maximum temperature recorded was 55°C (131°F). Some idea of the effort required to push through the mountains can be gained from the recorded facts about the drills used to bore the blasting holes. A 23.6 inch (60 cm) bit was kept in use until it had been worn down to a length of about 3 inches (8 cm), when it was changed for a new one – and this might be done as many

ABOVE Workers in the Simplon tunnel use hydraulic drills to bore twelve holes; this work took about two and a half hours, after which the holes were packed with dynamite and detonated.

as 400 times in a single day. The workings were inundated more than once, but the work went relentlessly forward until, on 19 May 1906, amid great celebrations, the tunnel was officially opened by King Victor Emmanuel III of Italy and M. Forrer, President of the Swiss Federation.

A CLASH OF INTERESTS

After the expenditure of so much effort and money, no one was about to grant running rights through the tunnel without a good deal of hard bargaining. For Wagons-Lits, the tunnel offered the exciting prospect of a brand new route for the Orient Express, down to Venice, then on to Trieste and Laibach (now Ljubljana), to join the existing route at Belgrade. The idea at once ran into opposition from Germany and Austria-Hungary. In particular, the Austrian government decreed that no foreign-operated train could pass through their territory – which included Trieste – without calling in at Vienna. It made no sense in terms of a unified rail network for Europe, but all too clearly reflected the clash of national interests, and rivalries between north and south, and east and west Europe. A less ambitious route was then proposed, to run from Paris via

Lausanne to Milan. This proved acceptable, and in the winter of 1906, the Simplon Express made its first journey. Two years later, the route was extended to Venice, whose splendid buildings at least hinted at the Orient and the splendours of Byzantium. By 1912, there was to be a further extension to Trieste, but beyond that Austrian intransigence barred the way. The Simplon Express was not yet quite ready to be christened the Simplon-Orient Express. One other important connection was made at the same time, when passengers travelling from London via Calais were given their place on the timetable.

It was almost as complex an operation as that of the original Orient Express had been. The line from Calais to Paris was the responsibility of the French Nord railway company. Passengers moving onward from Paris were handed over to the care of the Paris-Lyon-Méditerranée company. Their journey began at the Gare de Lyon, a building in the very blowsiest of Second Empire styles. Those with time to spare, having admired the architecture, could then sample the very considerable delights of the station restaurant, rated as one of the best in Paris, its loyalty to the traditions of Wagons-Lits evident in its name, Le Train Bleu. At the border town of Pontarlier, responsibility passed to the Swiss Federal Railway, whose section, which included the tunnel itself, ended at Iselle in Italy. The final section to Trieste was in the care of the Italian State Railways. With so many different interests involved, great care had to be taken not to give offence. In spite of the divided responsibility for the track, and the different locomotives provided for each section, the Simplon Express, as far as the passengers were concerned, was a through train, and they expected to stay in the same compartment and be looked after by the same staff throughout the journey. But what nationality should the staff be, and what language should they speak? It was formally decreed that staff should be employed in strict accordance with the track miles in each of the three countries: 467 miles (752 km) worth of staff should be French, 148 miles (239 km) Swiss, and 259 miles (417 km) Italian – and the language problem was solved by requiring the staff to be fluent in all appropriate languages. Perhaps there was no company in the world better able to meet such rigorous requirements than Wagons-Lits.

Running the Orient Express and the Simplon Express was a complex affair that went smoothly, simply because everyone in the chain of command knew exactly what was required of them, and where their duties started and ended. Work began with the preparation of the train for its journey. This was the

BELOW The Simplon tunnel in 1906, shortly before completion, with the service tunnel visible on the left. On the road is the mail coach, which until then had represented express travel across the Alps.

responsibility of the *controleurs* (controllers), who were permanently based in their offices at the various termini and at important intermediary stations. They had workmen under them who could look after minor repairs, such as a broken lock or a cracked window pane, but their main concern was to ensure the train was in perfect condition, with everything in the right place at the start of the journey. When a train arrived at a terminus, the empty cars were passed to the *baggagistes-nettoyeurs* (baggage-handlers-cleaners). The coaches were taken off to the sheds, and when they were returned to the station, they were in immaculate condition, with all the necessary clean linen and equipment on board. The cleaners returned with the cars and adopted their other role as baggage-handlers, responsible for collecting hand luggage from the porters and stowing it away in the correct compartment. Cleaners do not generally enjoy a very high status in any organisation, but these men – and it was an all-male work force – were supplied with smart, military-style uniforms, in the regulation dark blue of Wagons-Lits. In winter, like all the other staff, they were issued with greatcoats, which were to be worn when out on the platform.

Once the train was back in the station, responsibility fell on the *chef de brigade*, later known as the *chef de train*, a post for which there is no real modern equivalent. He was in charge of both the sleeping cars and the dining cars, which effectively made him the manager of a hotel on wheels. He not only oversaw the working of the train, but saw personally to the welfare of the most important guests. Only the truly grand qualified for this VIP treatment – nothing less than royalty or head of state would do.

The dining car was the fiefdom of the *maître d'hôtel*, a resplendent frock-coated figure, with a small army of head waiters, waiters and kitchen staff at his command. The *serveurs-receveurs* (waiters) were generally required to wear white coats – not a very practical uniform on a train hauled by a coal-fired locomotive equipped with a coal-burning kitchen range. As it was unthinkable that a waiter would appear in anything other than spotless attire, a blue uniform was also available. Out of sight, but vital to the whole operation, was the chef, with his kitchen staff. As it had done from the very start, Wagons-Lits made immense efforts to secure the services of the finest chefs – and whatever the regulations about internationalism, there was never any doubt about which nation ruled in this department. It was almost an article of faith that the best chefs in the world were French. So good were these masters of cuisine that attempts were constantly being made to tempt them away with

RIGHT Uniforms of around 1910: 1 and 2, chefs de train; 3 and 4, waiters; 5 and 6, maîtres d'hôtel; 7 and 8, porters and cleaners; 9 and 10, chefs de brigade; 11 and 12, head waiters; 13 and 14, sleeping car attendants; 15 and 16, conductors and controllers.

ternationale des Wagons-Lits

Grands Express européens

AGENTS DU SERVICE DE L'EXPLOITATION

offers from the finest restaurants – but so well were they cared for by Wagons-Lits that they never went. Even the lure of working as private chef for one of the most famous gourmets – and gourmands – in Europe, King Edward VII, could not persuade one cook to abandon his poky, inconvenient, travelling kitchen on the Orient Express.

The *conducteurs* (conductors), who had charge of the sleeping cars, may not have been at the top of the official hierarchy, but for many passengers they were the most important people on the train – with the possible exception of the chef. Their official duties were clearly laid out, and they were required to stay in the cars from the time they were handed

over by the cleaners at the start of the journey until they were handed back at the end. But it was well known that they were also available for unofficial duties, most commonly procuring suitable 'companions' for wealthy passengers, which was certainly the most lucrative. Far more important than what they did was what they did not do. In the small, enclosed world of

the train, liaisons and secret meetings could be kept from the eyes of the world at large, but could hardly escape the notice of the conductors. Everyone knew that the discretion of the Orient Express conductors could be relied upon, but that did not obviate the need to offer a handsome tip to make doubly sure. The conductors' lives were not easy; they were constantly on the move, and had to endure confined and not very comfortable quarters, but they were the envy of other railway workers.

Largely unseen, and generally forgotten, were the *brigadiers-postiers* (mail-guards), who were in charge of the *fourgons*. It was a responsible job, if unglamorous. Yet in the company's eyes, it was of great importance. A substantial amount of revenue came from carrying mail and packages, and it was imperative that the right package was set down at the right station, with all the necessary paperwork completed. In the early years of the Orient Express, this had not always been well managed. Packets had been left at the wrong stations or, worst of all, entirely lost. The establishment of the mail-guards put an end to those problems.

These were the staff who ensured the smooth running of the trains, and it's clear that there were quite enough posts to go around among the different nationalities. After World War I, some of the names changed, but the duties remained essentially the same. Yet even the most successful organisation will fail to meet the demands of its clientele, unless the staff have the initiative to bend the rules when the situation demands it. This was especially true of the Orient Express, where the passengers were often men and women who were used to having their every whim obeyed. They were paying a great deal of money and expected the same standard of service that they received at home, in mansion and in palace.

WEALTH AND INFLUENCE

The Maharajah of Cooch Behar, now Koch Bihar, in north east India was a man of vast wealth. He was also a man of importance, for although the state he ruled was small, it was considered of strategic importance to the British, because it lay under the shadow of the mountains of Tibet. In the early 1900s, there were endless rumours of Russian agents at work in Tibet, and every effort had to be made to keep the rulers of the border states happy, hence the Maharajah's journey to attend a conference in London in 1907. The Wagons-Lits personnel were as aware of delicate international situations as any diplomat, and were prepared to do their best to look after the Maharajah throughout his journey on the Orient Express.

LEFT Luggage being loaded under the watchful eye of the mail-guard at the Gare Maritime, Calais. The fourgon has the modernised badge of Wagons-Lits, though still based on the two initial letters, W. L.

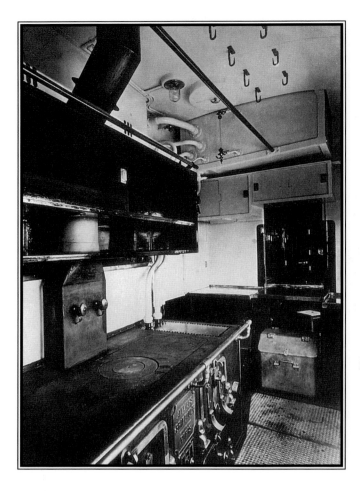

ABOVE Gourmet meals had to be produced under the most difficult conditions in cramped kitchens. This car from the 1930s still has a solid-fuel range; pots were hung from the ceiling, and utensils suspended from the rail above the range.

RIGHT It is a mark of the prestige of the Orient Express that some of Europe's finest chefs chose to work onboard the train in preference to luxury restaurants or private residences.

The Maharajah's demands were considerable, for he proposed to travel, not just with officials and advisers, but with all his wives and concubines as well. Two cars had to be completely refurbished: out went bunks and conventional seats, in came oriental divans and floor cushions, all draped in gold-embroidered cloth. The arrival of the Maharajah's private yacht at Constantinople was an affair of considerable interest, as he was followed down the gangplank by the ladies of the court, dressed in the most elegant and delicate of saris. All went well on the outward journey as the party relaxed in almost tropical luxury, courtesy of the salons' efficient heating system. But on the return, the heaters simply stopped working; the temperature plummeted, and the ladies began shivering in the cold, against which their flimsy silks offered no protection. Extra blankets

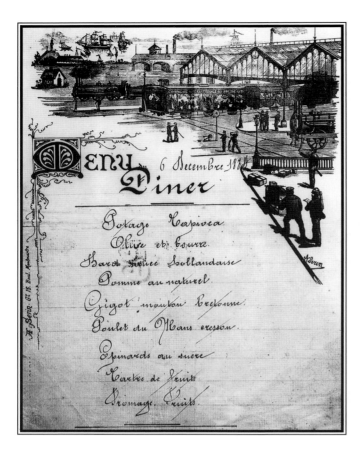

LEFT Wagons-Lits printed standard menu cards, onto which each day's bill of fare was written by hand.

BELOW LEFT This splendidly attired conductor displays Wagons-Lits' characteristic helpfulness and efficiency as he takes a little girl's ticket.

BELOW From the very beginning, the carriage of mail was an important source of revenue for Wagons-Lits.

were produced, but proved insufficient, so that conductors had to do the rounds of the other passengers, borrowing whatever clothing they could. It must have been a bizarre sight to see this specially created oriental salon full of ladies huddled in tweed overcoats and furs.

That problem solved, another now presented itself. The Orient Express chefs prided themselves on providing whatever dishes their clients demanded. Kosher and halal meals were commonplace and the chefs – admittedly with considerable

distaste – even went so far as to provide one ascetic English financier with his unalterable diet of soufflés and dry biscuits throughout the long journey. The Maharajah's passion, however, was for spicy lamb. Now, because of the delays in attempting to repair the heating system, the train was running late, extra meals were needed, and the kitchen was wholly bereft of lamb. Here was a dilemma indeed – no lamb and no scheduled stop before dinner time. The *chef de brigade* rose to the occasion. Company policy decreed that no unauthorised stops should ever be made,

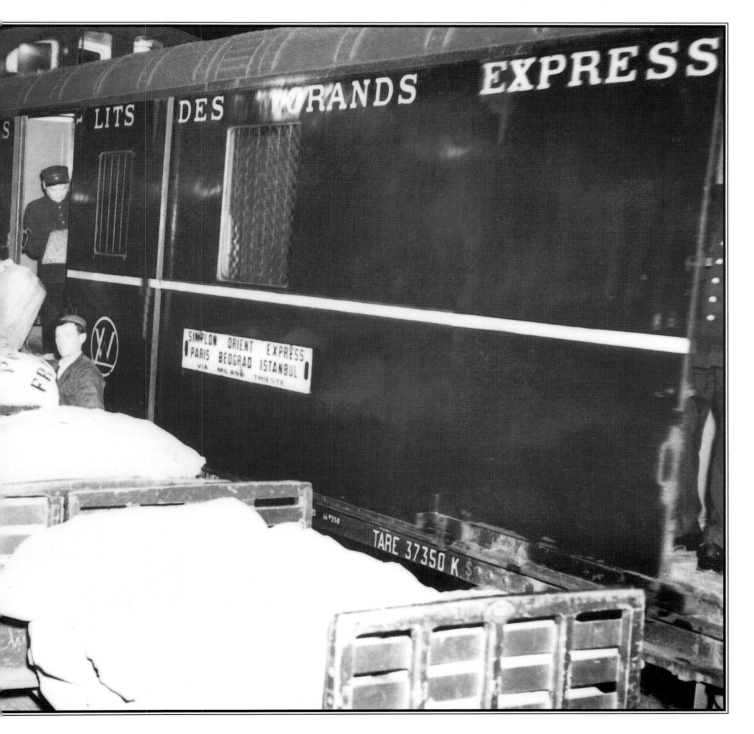

ABOVE Having movable furniture in dining cars and salons meant that a carriage could be transformed to meet the requirements of anyone powerful and rich enough to demand it.

but company laws would have to take second place to a Maharajah's wishes. The train was halted, a man was sent running off to a local butcher, and the day was saved. It was said that at the end of that journey, the Maharajah, instead of tipping the staff with the usual banknotes, passed out a handful of precious jewels.

Although the major event of the 1900s was the establishment of the Simplon Express, the original Orient Express was not neglected. The constant improvement to rolling stock was continued. The new generation of dining cars was even better sprung and had larger windows for those not entirely engrossed by the magnificent cuisine. An area was set aside in each car, fitted out with armchairs, where diners could be served with drinks before meals, or relax over coffee and brandies before retiring for the night. In the salons, louvred windows could be angled so that the

passengers could let air into a compartment without the accompaniment of smoke from the engine. Genuine night lights were provided in sleepers for the first time. In the old days, anyone wanting to keep a dim light drew a curtain across the space in front of the gas mantle, an action that would have given a safety officer, had such an official existed, a fit of apoplexy. Life on board was not just more comfortable, it was also a good deal safer. It would not be unreasonable to say that there was no railway company anywhere in the world that could surpass the service on this line, and very few that even attempted to match it. And this was reflected in the increasing demand for tickets.

In 1900, the Orient Express ran a daily service to Vienna, a train every Friday to Constanta with a guaranteed boat connection to Constantinople, and through trains to Constantinople on Wednesdays and Sundays. All these services were advertised with connections from London. On the outward journey from Paris, trains from Calais brought London passengers for a connection at Châlons-sur-Marne, while on the return journey, British passengers left at Strasbourg for Ostend. By 1909, however, the daily runs had been extended as far as Budapest, with two trains a week to

BELOW From the first, modest 1883 train, the first fifteen years of the Orient Express saw an increase in vehicle size to meet increasing demand, with an additional sleeping car being added by 1909.

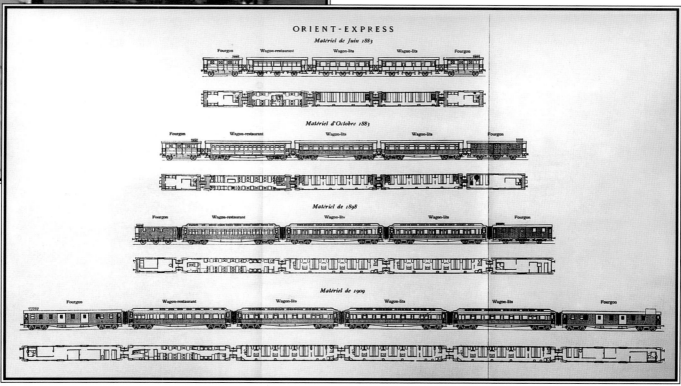

Constanta and three on the through line. The service was noted for its reliability, but no transport system in the world has ever been completely accident free, and this was no exception. One misadventure, which could have had appalling consequences, fortunately ended on a rather surreal note. On a December day in 1901, customers were sitting around in the station restaurant at Frankfurt. This was a splendid, high-ceilinged, panelled room, with no expense spared in decorative details, from marble pillars to ornate chandeliers. It was an establishment made for serious eating, the sort of place where one would not expect anything more disastrous than a corked bottle of wine. On this day, however, diners glancing up from their meal suddenly became aware that the Orient Express was heading straight for them at considerable speed and showing no signs of slowing down. They scattered as the engine leaped the tracks, hurtled through the end wall, and finally came to rest among a pile of rubble and smashed furniture. And there, hissing as gently as a kettle in the kitchen, it sat as the crowds gathered to see the strange phenomenon of a steam locomotive in the middle of a smart restuarant. Miraculously, there were no serious injuries. Like the accident described earlier (see p.35), it was to the considerable credit of the company that, in spite of the brake failure, which was in any case the responsibility of the company running the locomotive, its coaches survived being part of a train that had just demolished a considerable portion of a main line railway station. The accident certainly did nothing to deter passengers from using the train, which was becoming increasingly popular. Apart from attracting wealthy travellers, it was also finding favour with government agents, both official and clandestine.

THE 'SPOOK' EXPRESS

During the early years of the twentieth century, the Balkans played centre stage to any number of political dramas, and positively seethed with conspiracies and international jostlings for power. In 1908 alone, the 'Young Turks' forced through constitutional changes in Constantinople, King Ferdinand declared Bulgaria to be an independent nation, and Austria annexed Bosnia. Everything seemed to be in a state of permanent turmoil. It meant a constant shifting in the balance of power, and governments across Europe were eager to glean whatever information they could about the various factions struggling for supremacy or forging new alliances. The one and only train that ran right through the heart of the region was an obvious attraction for all those with a vested interest in

RIGHT *Wagons-Lits advertised their trains as representing the ultimate in luxury travel, as these table settings — as immaculate as any to be found in the world's finest hotels — confirm.*

collecting and passing on intelligence. It was used officially for the important work of carrying diplomatic bags. British King's Messengers, highly respectable retired officers, made the journey on a regular basis, sometimes as often as once a fortnight. Compartments were reserved for them throughout the year, and in these the diplomatic couriers travelled in solitary, but watchful, comfort. It was considered very good business by the

Orient Express, since the income was guaranteed, whether anyone used the reserved compartment or not.

Far more interesting were those whose status was definitely not recorded in any official documents, and whose reservations were certainly never made by government departments – the spies. One of the best known of these, though not necessarily for his espionage work, was Robert Baden-Powell, later the

ABOVE The Orient Express, seen here steaming towards Constantinople around 1910, was still quite modest in size, with just two sleeping cars, a restaurant car and only thirty-two passengers.

RIGHT Despite the elaborate decoration of this 1904 salon, the seating is, oddly, far from uniform, with a mixture of styles and materials, as well as single and double seats.

RIGHT This coach, part of the London express waiting in Paris, shows just how distinctive the Wagons-Lits livery was. The emblem was worked in brass, and shines out against the glossy royal blue of the coachwork.

founder of the Boy Scout movement. He had been a soldier in Afghanistan, but in later years became what was officially described as an 'assistant military secretary'. His fellow officers might have wondered why he was allowed to devote his time to his unusual hobby of tracking and recording rare moths and butterflies in remote regions of eastern Europe. He became a regular traveller on the Orient Express, frequently stopping off for butterfly-hunting expeditions, and returning with wonderfully intricate, coloured drawings of some remarkable specimens. They were drawings that would certainly have baffled lepidopterists, for the beautiful wing markings had never been seen on any known insect. They were, in fact, coded diagrams of military installations. The British War Office was matched in terms of spies on the train by the French Deuxième Bureau. While the British spies travelled undetected under a cloak of eccentricity, the French hid behind urbanity and sophistication. Just as no one ever questioned an Englishman flitting round Europe with a butterfly net, so no one thought twice about a French gentleman, accompanied by an attractive young lady who was clearly not his wife, stopping off and mooning around remote, romantic spots.

FEMME FATALE

Virtually all the spies and agents who made good use of the Orient Express were professionals in the service of their governments. In fiction, if less frequently in fact, the really fascinating figure is the international spy, buying and selling information wherever there was a market. It is often difficult to sort out reality from romantic myth, and of no one was this more true than a young Dutch woman, Margaretha Gertrud Zelle. Born in 1876, she married a Dutch officer of Scottish descent, Rudolph Macleod. His posting to Java enabled her to flee a life of drab provincialism, but the marriage was not a success. Mme Macleod took herself off to Paris, where she offered her services as an oriental dancer. There might not have been a great demand for her 'authentic Javanese' dances until she explained that part of the authenticity involved dancing in the nude. She seems to have been the first ever to dance naked on the Parisian stage, and she was soon starring at the Folies Bergères under a bogus Javanese name – Mata Hari.

Now notorious, she was soon enjoying the attentions of wealthy admirers and influential lovers in many countries. One of her most successful tours took her on the Orient Express to

Vienna and Bucharest, a journey that also brought her a new lover, Baron von Krohn, one of the heads of the German secret service. If a famous *femme fatale*, travelling the luxury trains of Europe in the company of such men of influence as Messimy, the French minister of war, was bound to attract attention – then this was doubly true of one who could count among her many lovers a leader of the German intelligence service. If she was a spy, then no spy in history has ever done so little to keep it a secret. Mata Hari was arrested in France and eventually executed by firing squad in 1917. It is ironic that when so many professional spies were regularly travelling on the Orient Express, one of the very few we know about who suffered the death penalty was probably never a spy at all.

International tensions permeated everything in the Balkans, even disrupting the smooth running of the region's most famous train. In June 1914, a Serbian guard boarded the train and demanded to know of the *chef de brigade* whether or not King Ferdinand of Bulgaria was on board. The *chef de brigade* prevaricated, saying that his name was certainly on the passenger list, but he was not aware of his actually having joined the train. Even the dimmest Serbian soldier would not have believed that a Wagons-Lits *chef de brigade* would be ignorant of the fact that he had royalty under his care. The guard

proceeded, peremptorily, to search all the compartments, to the considerable indignation of the passengers. Then he reached a set of compartments that were securely locked, at which he took the pass key and tried to push his way in. He was forcibly removed by one of the king's bodyguards, and it took a good deal of diplomacy on the part of the train staff to calm everyone down. The guard left, threatening dire reprisals against the staff, the *chef de brigade* in particular. This incident might well have led to a full-blown diplomatic row, had it not been quickly overtaken by events. A week later, on 28 June 1914, Archduke Franz Ferdinand of Austria was assassinated at Sarajevo by a Serbian student.

This was the event that was to spark off the Great War, but the conflict did not blaze up immediately. There was a confused period of a few weeks, full of accusations and counter-accusations, during which European rail travel somehow survived, if in considerably truncated form. On 28 July, Wagons-Lits announced that it could no longer run a full service on the Orient Express, and that Budapest was now the end of the line. Even that limited service was soon brought to an end when, just three days later, Germany declared war on France. One immediate result, a minor matter when set against the slaughter that was about to be unleashed, was the

It was not only in fiction that spies and agents travelled the Orient Express. The most famous of them all was the exotic dancer Mata Hari, seen here with considerably more clothing than she wore in her stage act. She was accused of working for the Germans during the war and was executed by the French in 1917.

FACING PAGE In January 1901, the train jumped the rails and charged into the crowded restaurant hall at Frankfurt's Central Station. Astonishingly, no one was seriously injured, though the opulent restaurant suffered the almost complete demolition of one wall.

ABOVE The 'train de luxe militaire', which ran from Paris to Warsaw after the end of World War I. The train, which had a tricolour painted on it, avoided travelling through Germany.

BELOW It is 22 June 1940, and Hitler is climbing aboard the famous Wagons-Lits carriage No. 2419 in which the German military officially conceded defeat in 1918.

seizure by Germany of all Wagons-Lits rolling stock in its territory, a total of sixty-four dining cars and thirty-five sleeping cars. The proud name of Wagons-Lits was removed, and in its place went that of the German sleeping car company, Mitteleuropäischeschlafwagengesellschaft – later mercifully shortened to 'Mitropa' – a new Orient Express line was inaugurated from Berlin to Constantinople, and renamed the Der Balkaner Zug (The Balkan Train).

It was a sad time for Wagons-Lits, but they had revenge of a kind in 1918 at Compiègne, where Marshal Foch and representatives of the Allies accepted the German surrender in restaurant car No. 2419. In time, the wheel was to come full circle. In June 1940, Hitler ordered the same car to be taken to the same spot, and now it was his turn to accept the surrender of the French forces. After that, it was hauled away to Berlin and put on exhibition until 1944. Then, when it became clear that Germany was losing the war, Hitler ordered the car to be blown up. There were to be no more scenes of humiliation in Car No. 2419. But, to return to 1918, the end of the Great War found the Orient Express on the brink of what many would consider to be its glory years. For Wagons-Lits, they were to be years beset with problems and difficulties.

ABOVE Marshal Foch, second from the right, and the other signatories to the Armistice Convention pose by the steps to
dining car No. 2419 on 30 November 1918.

The Simplon-Orient Express in Switzerland. The steam engine has made way for the far more efficient, though admittedly much less romantic, electric locomotive.

CHAPTER FOUR

Turmoil and Change

No one seriously expected that rail services would return to normal as soon as the war ended. Nevertheless, it was considered a subject of great importance, and the particular need to re-establish international routes as a way of moving towards a more united, peacetime Europe was specifically set out in the Treaty of Versailles (1919). Nagelmackers had been forced to tour the capitals of pre-war Europe, wheedling, cajoling and arguing to acquire running rights. Now the situation was very different. There was strong international pressure on Dalziel and Wagons-Lits to resume services just as soon as was practically possible. But there could be no simple road to restoration, for the political map had changed beyond all recognition.

The old Austro-Hungarian Empire had gone for ever, and a series of brand-new states had taken its place, each with its own particular response to the international world in which it now had to make its way. Yugoslavia, for example, was very keen to form strong bonds with the West, while Hungary looked East, and declared itself a Soviet Republic in 1919. The other new Soviet Republic, Russia, was in these early years preoccupied with establishing its own internal security. The situation in Turkey was very far from being resolved. The Ottoman Empire had aligned itself with Germany in the war, and was now faced with partition as a real possibility. At the same time, a new man had appeared on the scene, determined to change the country for ever, and in every way. Out would go the old Ottoman state and its hierarchies, and in its place a modern, independent, western-style state would be built. That man was Kemal Ataturk. The Great War was over: civil war in Turkey was about to begin. Germany was defeated, and was, for a time at least, to be a pariah rather than a partner in the new Europe that was being built on the ruins of the old. All these factors played an important, and in some cases a decisive, part in discussions on international rail travel.

TRAIN DE LUXE MILITAIRE

One thing was very clear: there was no way, at the end of 1918, that the Orient Express could simply be reinstated. The first move towards restoring railway normality came from the military, anxious to ensure that the victors would be unimpeded on their journeys across the continent. In February 1919, the French minister of war organised the Train de Luxe Militaire, strictly reserved for high-ranking officers and VIPs. It ran from Paris via Vienna, Warsaw and Prague to Bucharest. But there was an equally urgent need to restore something like normality to ordinary

RIGHT *The Simplon-Orient Express at Milan in the 1930s en route from Paris to Istanbul. The photograph gives some idea of the thousands of tons of steel used in the station's construction.*

BELOW *The Wagons-Lits travel agency at Timisoara in Romania in 1925. As well as advertising the usual luxury trains, it also promotes the trains bleus.*

European relations, to provide lines of communication between capitals, to restore economic dialogue and, just as importantly, to ensure freedom of movement, which would send out a clear signal that the continent was, indeed, at peace again. It was time to restore the *trains de luxe* to the tracks.

A conference was held in Paris in March, 1919, organised by the French, but with the active encouragement of other governments, including the Swiss, Dutch, Italian and Yugoslav. The aim was to establish the long-term future of international trains and their routes. At the heart of the proposals was the newly named Simplon-Orient Express. In general terms, the aim was to provide a link that would stretch from London, through Calais or Boulogne, to the Orient. There was no question of sending trains through Germany. As before the war, trains were to make their way south through France and Switzerland, via the Simplon tunnel and from Milan to Venice and Trieste. But this would no longer be the end of the line: the

route would continue through the brand new kingdom of Yugoslavia to Laibach (now Ljubljana), Zagreb and on to Vincovce (now Vinkovci). Here, the train would divide, one part going to Bucharest and Constanta, the other to Athens via Thessalonika. And there was to be a new daily link, the Bordeaux-Milan Express, which would be mainly made up of Wagons-Lits cars, but with the addition of an ordinary first-class carriage.

Milan had suddenly acquired considerable importance in the European rail system, and plans were at once put in hand for a new station. The foundation stone was duly laid, but a decade was to pass before Milan Central, the biggest station in the world, covering 103 acres (42 hectares), was completed. It was a most remarkable building, of two seemingly unrelated parts. The main entrance, concourse and booking hall are grandiloquence taken to extremes, a riot of stained glass windows and marbled walls. It was aptly summed up by Jeffrey Richards and John M. MacKenzie in their book, *The Railway Station*: 'The

BELOW *A simple but effective luggage label, printed in red and green. With an increasing number of routes being run by Wagons-Lits, each named express was given its own distinctive label.*

ABOVE *By the 1930s, the Orient Express was operating a line running from Nis in Serbia to Athens, seen here crossing the spectacular Gorgopotamos Bridge near the Albanian border.*

whole thing had the feel of a palace of some mad potentate, a train-obsessed, latter-day equivalent of Ludwig of Bavaria'. Yet behind it, the train shed is an uncompromisingly modern structure of exposed steel and glass. Whatever else it might be, the station, designed to be the pivotal point for the Orient Express, was certainly memorable.

There was no chance of the full service set out in the conference being implemented immediately, as more time was needed to restore war-damaged rolling stock and repair the infrastructure. Nevertheless, on 10 April 1919, Wagons-Lits published the timetable for the first run of the Simplon-Orient Express. The journey started in London at 8.50 a.m., with passengers reaching Paris Nord at 7.30 p.m. the same day. They then crossed Paris to join the train at the Gare de Lyon for the connection to Milan, which arrived at 2.40 p.m. the following day. Meanwhile, the other new express was to leave Bordeaux, just before the London train at 7.30 a.m., and then steam across France to Lyon and the Mont Cenis tunnel, reaching Milan a few minutes ahead of the Simplon-Orient. The united parties

now had an eight-and-a-half hour journey to Trieste. Here, they had to change trains for a long haul of thirteen hours by way of Zagreb to Vincovce, where there was a further parting of the ways, one section continuing to Bucharest and the other to Belgrade. The Paris train was made up of two *fourgons*, four sleeping cars and one dining car. The Bordeaux train was altogether more modest, the Wagons-Lits contribution being limited to one sleeping car and one dining car. But it was a start.

There was still a magic attached to the name of the Orient Express, but the reality fell a long way short of the sumptuous glories associated with the earlier years. Much of the rolling stock was in poor condition, and there was no sign of the German sleeping car company, Mitropa, being in any hurry to hand back the cars that had been confiscated. Wagons-Lits had to wait until 1922, and then got back no more than a third of what they had lost. In the meantime, the workshops did what they could to hold the ageing cars together. They worked valiantly, but it was always something of a relief to passengers in those early post-war years if the car in which they started a

RIGHT *The remarkably decorative toilet compartment of a 1920s S-class coach. The marble-topped washstand gives it a rather old-fashioned look.*

journey wasn't withdrawn for some fault or other before the end of it. Everyone had shown commendable enthusiasm for the new routes at the Paris conference, but there was no sign of that enthusiasm being translated into any sense of urgency on the ground. Work on replacing old track in Romania and Yugoslavia advanced at a frustratingly slow pace. It was not until well into 1920 that the Simplon Express could really justify the addition of Orient to its name. The route to Constantinople was reopened via Sofia, and the train was split at Nis with one set of coaches heading south via Thessalonika to Athens.

The Wagons-Lits empire was slowly spreading, and not just in terms of route miles. Dalziel was now very much the man in charge. A new company had been formed in Britain, the Pullman Car Company, and he was at once appointed chairman. It took over the stock of the old British Pullman Car Company, and was now totally independent of the original American concern. At that time, there were seventy-four Pullman cars in Britain, and Dalziel had contracts with a number of different railway companies. These included the London, Brighton & South Coast Railway, the line that was to see the running of the most famous of all British Pullmans, the *Brighton Belle*. Dalziel's most important change was to bring all future coach building to Britain, and it was not long before British companies were also manufacturing for Wagons-Lits. The two companies, which had begun as rivals, were now working together in close partnership to their mutual advantage. And expansion had not yet come to an end. All the new routes and the proposed improvements meant nothing unless there was a regular supply of passengers to buy the tickets. What the Wagons-Lits-Pullman consortium needed was an organistaion that could deliver passengers for their trains. They found just what they wanted in the oldest tour operator of them all.

ENTER THOMAS COOK

In 1841, a young man organised an excursion for 570 passengers who were taken in open trucks on a 12 mile (19 km) journey on part of the infant British railway system. They left Leicester for a temperance meeting at Loughborough, not quite the sort of journey likely to interest the men at Wagons-Lits. But just five years later, the young man had built up an organisation that was running pleasure excursions throughout the country. His name was Thomas Cook. By 1855, he was sending parties off to Europe and, by 1866, America had been added to the tourist itinerary. He was also responsible for inventing and introducing that most useful aid to the tourist in

LEFT *By the 1920s, single compartments had become very compact. This photograph shows one in daytime mode, but with the washstand folded down and the cupboard open.*

foreign lands – the traveller's cheque. As Thomas Cook and Son, the business flourished, and Dalziel was only too delighted to take the opportunity when it arose of buying it up to complete the trio of companies. As Cook-Wagons Lits, they now had some four hundred travel offices spread around the world. The new organisation was ideally placed to sell tickets for luxury trains to meet a growing demand for exotic holidays – all they needed to do was bring back the luxury. This was never going to be an easy task, and their efforts were constantly hampered by new problems that arose all the time, generally in areas where the company had no control.

By 1920, there was a general feeling that the time had come to release Austria and Germany from their isolation, to stop treating them as the bad boys of Europe. The first good news for Wagons-Lits came in spring of that year, when Austria restored the running rights over its territory, rights that had first been negotiated when Nagelmackers had signed the contracts for the original Orient Express. This was not, however, good news for Mitropa, which seemed to be destined to operate only within its national borders. It did contrive to keep one important link open, the route from Berlin to the Hook of Holland, the port used by British ferries sailing out of Harwich. It was not quite the end of the affair. The loss of territory rankled with the German railway companies, who retaliated by banning the use of Wagons-Lits anywhere in their territory, insisting that only Mitropa cars could be used. Running a railway company in the 1920s suddenly required considerable diplomatic skill. Once again, it was not just a case of commercial transactions. National honour was at stake, and the professional diplomats inevitably became involved.

The arguments with Austria rattled on. Although Wagons-Lits had an agreement, the terms were such that it could be broken at any time, simply by handing over a written notice to that effect. It was not a situation in which long-term plans could be made with any confidence, and Wagons-Lits pressed hard for a better deal. The Austrians were reluctant to go any further in granting rights. It was clearly time for diplomatic pressure to be brought to bear. The French government was in the middle of negotiating a trade treaty with Austria, and, without actually making any threats, let it be known that the refusal to accommodate Wagons-Lits was doing nothing to help the Austrian cause. Dalziel was himself a man of considerable political influence, and he made quite sure that British pressure was also added. The Austrians knew that they stood to lose good will and trade connections with two of the most powerful countries in Europe, but at the same time, the rail networks of Austria and Germany were inexorably intertwined, and they were equally reluctant to antagonise their neighbour. It was Wagons-Lits that took the initiative in placating German

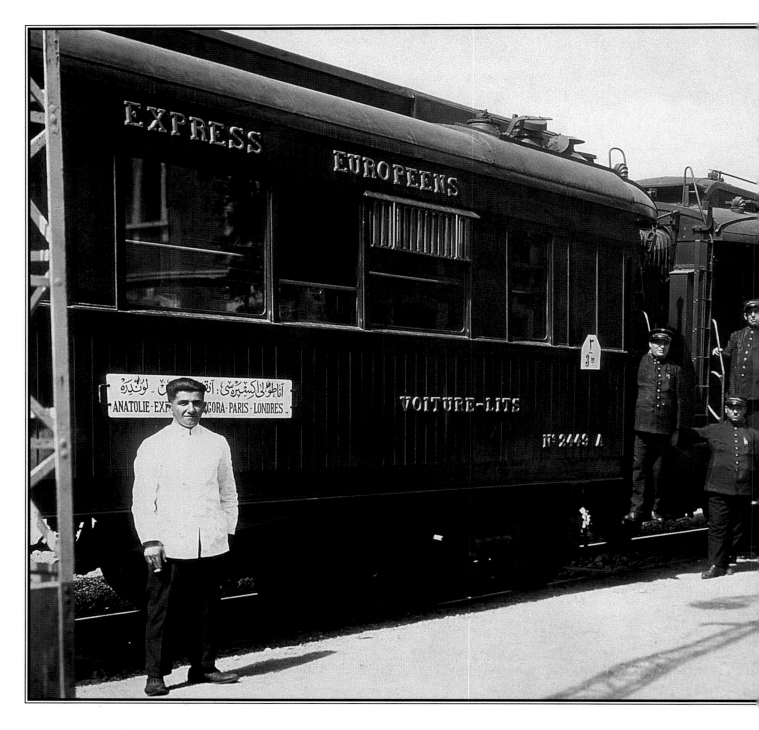

interests. It waived its claim to the 16 million francs Mitropa owed in compensation for grabbing its rolling stock – not such a generous gesture as it might seem, since Mitropa did not have 16 million francs anyway. The best that Wagons-Lits could have hoped for would have been to force Mitropa into bankruptcy, but that was not a very realistic option. In any case, Mitropa now had its own international conections, with a large part of the shares being held by the Great Eastern Railway in Britain, and by Canadian Pacific. This meant that its own trans-Europe route, from the Hook of Holland to Berlin, was secure. Dalziel

was not upset by this, for his Pullman coaches were being used for the London to Harwich boat train from the end of 1920. Mitropa also retained its own sleeping-car service with Austria. Eventually, agreement was reached, and the various companies could concentrate on running trains and improving services.

For Wagons-Lits, the first priority had to be rolling stock. Thanks to Dalziel, work could be speeded up by adding British factories to those of France and Belgium, an arrangement that soon proved its worth. The most important development was the introduction of all-steel coaches, initially to be supplied for

their final form, the sleeping cars had ten compartments, originally all singles, but upper berths were later added to allow passenger numbers to rise to sixteen or even twenty per car. With space at a premium, the toilet arrangements were neatly organised. Washrooms were sandwiched between two compartments, and could be entered from either. Anyone wanting a wash simply opened the door from their own compartment and, once inside, bolted the door opposite to ensure privacy – a system that worked well so long as everyone remembered to unlock the door before leaving. It was also, as quite a few romantics discovered, an ideal arrangement for a young lady and gentleman who could be respectably settled in their single compartments, with no one able to see an amorous figure slip from one to the other through the washroom.

RENÉ PROU AND THE ART DECO LOOK

Although the construction of the new carriages was completely modern, there was still an old-fashioned air to the compartments themselves, with their dark wood panelling. This was lightened by decorative details. In the English coaches, built either at Leeds or at Metropolitan Cammell in Birmingham, designers such as Morison and Nelson were engaged to produce some exquisite marquetry panels. These were generally very traditional, mostly using floral motifs. The coaches made in France and Belgium were fundamentally the same, but here decorators tended to favour a more modern, Art Deco approach. René Prou, perhaps the best known of them all, used very geometric patterns, and, instead of the soft blendings of marquetry, favoured the bold outlines produced by setting white plaster of Paris into the wood. The later carriages, from the end of the 1920s, were known as the LX, or luxury, class and certainly earned the name. In addition to the sleeping cars, there was a new set of dining cars, sharing the same construction and similarly decorated.

With its new rolling stock, the Orient Express in its various forms was offering a service that not only matched that of its first decades, but in many ways improved upon it. Journey times had been shortened and more routes were available. If the future looked uncertain, it was not because Wagons-Lits was lacking in self-confidence, but because of continuing political instability. The greatest worries were over the situation in Turkey, since that had always been the destination of the great train. This was resolved in October 1923 when a new republic was proclaimed with Kemal Ataturk as its first president. One potential difficulty, as far as train journeys were concerned, arose when it was announced that Constantinople would no

what was, officially, the Méditerranée Express, and popularly known as the Train Bleu, which aimed to meet the demand for fashionable holidays on the Côte d'Azur. At that time, the only company in the three countries that was able to take on the order was the Leeds Forge Company, England. In 1922, Dalziel placed an order for forty of what became S-type coaches, which would then be shipped to Europe from the new ferry terminal at Immingham on the east coast. The success of these steel coaches brought demands from other lines, especially the Orient Express, and soon a string of factories was at work. In

longer be the capital, and would indeed no longer be known as Constantinople but as Istanbul. The new capital was to be Angora, now Ankara, at the time little more than a collection of mud houses set in the middle of the Anatolian plain, on the Asian side of the Bosphorus. It was not a place to attract visitors, but it was the capital.

Ankara already had a railway, which had been built before the war in the years of international rivalry. Originally, this had been a largely German affair, part of a railway route intended to link Berlin with Baghdad, but which had never been completed. Now, however, it was to be included in the Wagons-Lits system, with the inauguration of the Anatolian Express, from Haydarpasa station on the east side of the Bosphorus to the new

capital. In the meantime, Turkey was going through a period of rapid change, most notably in the suppression of the influence of religious organisations on government. One victim was the best-known symbol of the old order, the fez, which was banned in 1925. Gentlemen, however, still felt that they needed hats, and it was said that for some time it was scarcely possible to move in the *fourgons* of the Orient Express, which were crammed with boxes full of all kinds of headgear, from toppers to flat caps. But the big question remained unanswered: Would

BELOW *This multicoloured map for 1930–31 shows the extent to which the Wagons-Lits empire had expanded, even if all the connections were not yet complete.*

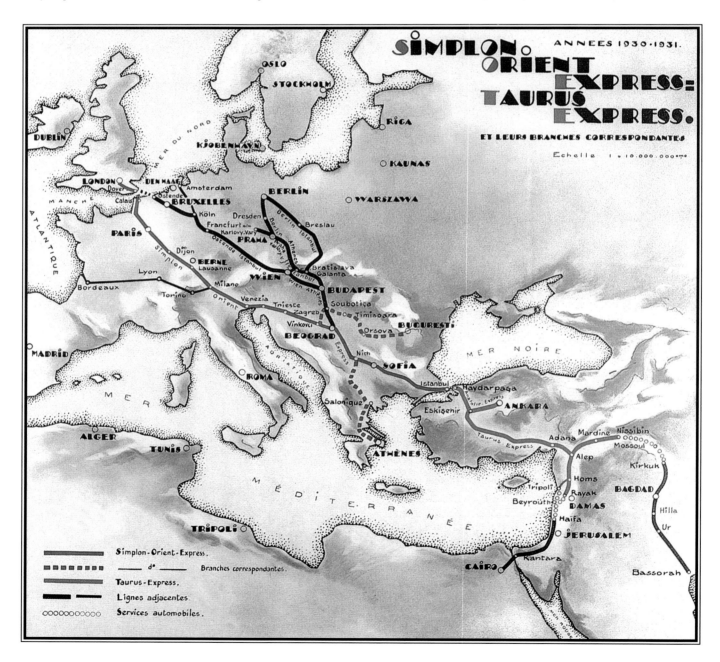

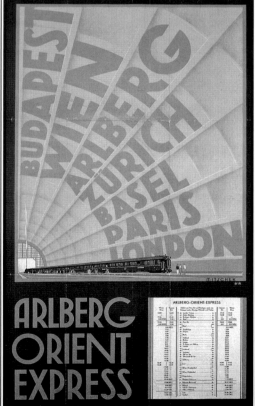

ABOVE *In 1923, in response to the changing political climate, the Orient Express was rerouted away from Germany to reach Austria through Switzerland and the Arlberg tunnel. The Arlberg-Orient Express is seen here steaming through Austria.*

LEFT *Wagons-Lits commissioned some of Europe's finest graphic artists for their posters. This 1930 example by Mitschek avoids the obvious appeal of alpine views, concentrating instead on the simple grandeur of modern stations.*

BELOW *The opening of the Simplon tunnel under the Alps in 1906 offered a new route to the Orient, but it was not until the 1920s that the Simplon-Orient Express covered the full route shown on the destinations board. By then Turkey had been through a revolution, and Constantinople had become Istanbul.*

LEFT *Today we are accustomed to standardised coaches, with every element fixed in place, but Wagons-Lits wanted to create the impression that the passengers were guests in a moving hotel.*

ABOVE *This Pullman lounge, circa 1926, is intended to convey a comfortable, homely feel with the floral motifs of the upholstery matching the marquetry panels.*

there be the same demand for tickets to a young republic that there had been for the capital of the Ottoman Empire? The answer was to be found by looking even further East.

One part of the triumvirate that now made up Wagons-Lits had more experience than any in this area. In the nineteenth century, Thomas Cook began running tourist excursions to the Middle East, to Egypt in particular, and they had proved extremely popular. But a huge boost to that popularity came in November 1922 when the archeologist Howard Carter opened up the tomb of Tutankhamun at Luxor. Wagons-Lits also had an interest in the area. As early as 1893, it had a restaurant car and two sleeping cars running between Cairo and Port Said, which in later years became the Cairo-Luxor Express. Now plans were put in hand to link the Orient Express and its eastern

cousin. The new route was to leave the line of the Anatolian express at Eskisehir and head for Aleppo (now Halab) in Syria. Here, the route was again to divide, one arm continuing east to Baghdad, and the other heading south via Beirut to Cairo. It was to be known as the Taurus Express.

When it opened in 1930, its route was, like that of the original Orient Express, still incomplete. But, unlike the travellers of the 1890s bumping over terrible mountain roads in cramped coaches, the new tourists would be carried a good deal more rapidly and more comfortably in motor vehicles. It proved a huge success, offering the splendours of the East in luxury, with famous monuments to enjoy, from the magnificent fortress of Aleppo to the pyramids of Egypt and the mosques of Baghdad. A poster of the time, published for the British market,

advertised London to Baghdad in eight days and guaranteed 'safety, rapidity, economy'. The Orient Express was linked to the Taurus Express by a special ferry service across the Bosporus, and at the height of its popularity, the Taurus service had sixty sleeping cars and twenty dining cars on its side of the water.

Changes were not limited to the East, and once again they were driven by politics. In January 1923, just when everything seemed to be settling down, France and Belgium, exasperated by what they saw as unreasonable delays in the payment of war reparations, marched their troops into the Ruhr. As part of its response, the German government once again withdrew running rights to foreign trains. At Wagons-Lits, the rail maps

of Europe had to be taken out again, and the hunt was on for yet another alternative route. The outcome was a service through France to Basel, then across Switzerland via Zurich to the Arlberg tunnel, and so into Austria. Thus yet another new train was born, the Arlberg-Orient Express. What had seemed at first as no more than a temporary solution to an irritating problem turned out to be something of a blessing. The new line proved very popular with Swiss businessmen, and was also the favoured route for delegates attending the League of Nations headquarters in Geneva. British interests were served by links to the line through either Calais or Boulogne. As a result, when the occupation of the Ruhr ended in 1924 and running rights were restored, the Arlberg route was retained. There was no longer just one Orient Express but a whole collection of them, and the system was soon rationalised and divided up. The plain, unadorned Orient Express still ran from Paris to what was now Istanbul, the Simplon served Belgrade, Bucharest and Sofia, the Arlberg terminated at Athens; and yet another line was added, the Ostend-Vienna-Orient Express. Between them, they offered a comprehensive service of luxury trains, linking Western Europe with the Balkans, with the added possibility of offering passengers the benefits of traditional Wagons-Lits comfort beyond the boundary of Europe and on into Asia.

The British weren't so euphoric. Passengers still had to make their way to a Channel port, get themselves and their luggage onto the ferry, and join the express on the other side of the Channel. Dalziel had tried to negotiate for a genuine train ferry operation earlier in the century, but had been thwarted by the British government. Attitudes had now changed, not least because that same government had recently been faced with the immense task of moving vast quantities of men and *matériel* into Europe. A regular train ferry was established in 1924 as an Anglo–Belgian venture, linking Harwich to Zeebrugge, but Dalziel's main concern was the short sea routes across the Channel. In 1924, he began the Continental Express from London to Dover, using a rake of new Pullman coaches, decked out in a fresh livery of chocolate and cream. A similar train was despatched across the Channel to continue the run from Calais to Paris. The full service began in 1926, and to commemorate the Golden Jubilee of Wagons-Lits, it was christened the Flèche d'Or (the Golden Arrow). Dalziel's dream of a single train running from London to Paris, using a train ferry on the short sea crossing, was not realised until 1936, eight years after his death in 1928. The Wagons-Lits coaches built for this Dover–Dunkerque night service, though scaled down to the tight British loading gauge, were nevertheless the largest and heaviest coaches to run on British metals.

Several years before that, the Wall Street crash of 1929 had sent western economies tumbling into the abyss. By 1931, the unthinkable had happened: second-class coaches were added to Pullman trains, even if the Orient Express still hung on to its old traditions. It was the first sign that the day of the luxury trains would not last for ever.

AN AUDIENCE WITH MISS BAKER

In many respects, the 1920s and 1930s were the glamour days of the Orient Express. To the list of the very wealthy, the business tycoons and aristocrats of pre-war years, there could now be added the new élite – the singers, dancers , actors and, the newest phenomenon of all, the movie stars. Among those remembered with particular affection by at least one conductor was the American cabaret artist, Josephine Baker, whose jazzy, erotic speciality was her 'banana dance', in which her costume consisted of no more than a few bananas hung from a string round her hips. It was very late one night, long after everyone had retired, that she called a conductor to her compartment and pleaded with him, as a special favour, to raid the kitchen and bring her a drink and a sandwich. Rather reluctantly he agreed, but probably thought it well worth the effort. He was about to be the one-man audience at a banana dance performance. She was later to win the respect of many of the Wagons-Lits staff, who remembered her for the help she gave in the aftermath of the greatest catastrophe that ever befell the Orient Express.

On the whole, the train had a very good safety record, though there was one serious accident on 6 November 1929. The train was running on the Paris–Istanbul route, travelling at

LEFT *The presence of film stars on Wagons-Lits trains added a touch of extra glamour to rail travel, and always made good publicity. Marlene Dietrich and Jean Marais acknowledge their fans.*

RIGHT *One of the most serious accidents in the history of the Orient Express occurred on 6 November 1929, just outside Vitry-le-François.*

full speed, about to pass the station of Vitry-le-François. It was a dark, foggy night, but the signals were all set in its favour, as the driver would have expected: the Orient Express had priority over almost anything else on the system. For some inexplicable reason, however, no one was aware that a local goods train had come to a halt on the main line, where it certainly had no right to be. The collision was unavoidable, for with the poor visibility there was no chance that the driver could have seen the obstruction in time to stop his train. Freight wagons, the express locomotive and tender tumbled down the embankment, dragging the *fourgon* after them. To the great good fortune of the passengers, the next coupling in the train was snapped and the cars all remained upright. The passengers were saved, but driver, fireman and one conductor were killed. The next calamity was no accident. On the night of 12 September 1931, the Orient Express had just left Budapest and was heading west across the Biatobargy viaduct when a bomb exploded. The locomotive and nine cars plunged down into the ravine; twenty people died instantly and many more were seriously injured. Most of the surviving passengers were either in a state of silent shock or having hysterics, as they took in the enormity of what had happened, and waited to be rescued. It was then that Josephine Baker, one of the passengers who had survived unscathed, stepped in to help. No exotic dance this time, but instead she gave an impromptu recital of her best known songs, ending with her personal hymn to Paris, 'J'ai deux amours'. Hungary at the time was a fascist state, and the bombing was at once condemned as a communist outrage. The authorities claimed

ABOVE *Stoppages for snow had always been a risk in winter, on the long journey through central Europe, but none was ever as severe as that of 1929. This snowbound party in 1920 seems to be quite enjoying the occasion.*

LEFT *In the vicious winter of 1929, a Simplon-Orient bound for Constantinople got stuck in a snowdrift for six miserable days.*

that Marxist slogans had been daubed at the site, and set about rounding up opponents of their regime. Then, to their great embarrassment, Austrian police arrested a Hungarian, Sylvester Matsuka, who had been caught preparing to bomb another railway location near Ansbach. Matsuka not only admitted responsibility for the Biatobargy bombing, but boasted about it. He was no Communist, but a member of the ultra-right Arrow Cross League, enthusiastic supporters of the fascist regime. He was eventually tried in secret in Hungary, and executed in 1936.

SNOWBOUND

One of the most famous incidents of those years was not really an accident, but could easily have become a tragedy. On the evening of 29 January 1929, the Simplon-Orient Express set off on its regular run to Istanbul. The weather was atrocious; few passengers had crossed the channel, and not many more had joined at Paris. As the train made its way across Europe, the conditions steadily deteriorated. Rivers were frozen, the temperature in central Europe had reached as low as -15°C (5°F), and fresh snow was falling, driven by strengthening winds.

The train struggled on to Vienna, where many of the passengers disembarked, and officials began to wonder if it was safe to continue much further. The new engine on the train was a powerful Austrian 4-6-0, which, with its six large, coupled driving wheels would, it was thought, shoulder its way through the worst the weather could bring. Everything went well as far as Budapest, where there was a conference between the officials of the railway operating company, the locomotive crew and the Wagons-Lits officials. There had been reports that the way ahead was blocked, but no one was sure how serious the situation really was as telephone communications were down. Wagons-Lits headquarters was generally in contact with all the outlying offices, and in theory were best placed to gauge the overall picture, so it was decided to leave the final decision to them. The *chef de train* managed to reach Paris by phone, where an official made it very clear that it would take more than winter weather, however bad, to stop the Orient Express.

So the train made its slow progress to the Turkish border, where there were even more alarming reports , but still no phones. There was no choice but to press on, following instructions from Paris, even though by now blizzards were ripping across the track. The driver reduced speed to a crawl, and sometimes had to stop altogether, reverse and take a running charge to burst through a snowdrift. Then, inevitably, a drift was reached that refused to yield

to the might of the locomotive. There was no going forward and no possibility of retreat. In reverse, the light wagon at the rear would be unlikely to survive an encounter with even a modest drift.

Not many of the passengers were aware at first of the seriousness of the situation, but the train crew certainly were. The temperature outside was far below zero, and everything depended on keeping a fire in the grate and a head of steam, not

to move the train but to keep the heating systems working. But on a large locomotive the steam has to be used or pressure will build inside the boiler. When working, this is no problem, but when standing still for long periods, steam has either to be blown off deliberately or allowed to escape through the safety valves. But in the sub-zero conditions, could anyone be sure that the essential valves would not simply freeze up and refuse to open? Then there was the question of whether fuel and water supplies might run out. No one knew how long it would be before relief arrived, but at least everyone was confident that there was no possibility that the authorities could overlook the non-arrival of the Orient Express. What the party stranded on the train had not allowed for was the general breakdown in communications across the whole area.

A survey of the stocks on board showed that there was enough food for two days, so there seemed no need for concern on that score. But two days passed and all that changed was the depth of snow outside, which looked terrifying but was, in fact, providing much-needed insulation from the biting wind. By the third day it was clear that more active measures were essential. Passengers joined the train staff in digging a tunnel out from the train, a task that proved incredibly difficult as the sides kept collapsing. Eventually, the chef and two of his helpers from the kitchen were able to get out and force their way through the snow in search of a village. It was the first foray for food, but not the last, as they persuaded local villagers to sell some of their own rather meagre supplies – at a price. But at least the passengers could be fed. The real cost was paid by the Wagons-Lits staff who went on the expeditions, wearing shoes intended for meandering down heated railway carriages, not for sub-zero temperatures and deep snow: they were all to suffer from frostbite. The attempt to provide heat via the engine had to be abandoned, as fuel supplies ran low, and what was left was reserved for the kitchen range and a small stove.

The situation was moving from unpleasant to desperate when, on the sixth day, soldiers appeared on sledges with much-needed supplies and the good news that they had not, as some were beginning to think, simply been forgotten. The following day, a plume of smoke along the track announced the arrival of the snow-plough engine. The locomotive was unfrozen, fuel piled in, water added to the boiler, and at last the journey to Istanbul was resumed. The passengers at least knew who they had to thank for their survival, and they all signed a testimonial to the staff, praising the 'superhuman' efforts they had made without any regard to personal health or safety. It ended with a phrase that in a way summed up the Wagons-Lits ethos – 'they had done their duty to the end'.

A LIFE OF CRIME

Happily, events such as these were a rarity, and most passengers on the luxury train enjoyed an uneventful trip. But in the popular fiction of the time, a journey on the Orient Express was never uneventful. The appeal of the train to fiction writers was obvious: they could assemble an international cast of characters, keep them confined to each other's company for days on end, as they moved from one exotic location to another. The most successful, in terms of sales, was Maurice Dekobra's *La Madone des Sleepings*, first published in 1927. This was no chaste Madonna: the heroine is first met dancing in the nude and subsequently spends her time divided between amorous affairs and foiling dastardly communist plots. A far more realistic view is provided, as one would expect, by Graham Greene in his 1932 novel, *Stamboul Train*. There are no real heroes and heroines here, but characters who might indeed have been found on the Orient Express: the philandering business man, with more than a hint of Zaharoff in his nature; the would-be revolutionary leader with no hope of success; and the not very good dancer, on her way to what will certainly prove to be a sleazy engagement in an Istanbul night club. The closed world of the train was absolutely perfect for the detective story, as Agatha Christie showed in *Murder on the Orient Express* (1933). Glamorous people and international intrigue, spiced up with a seasoning of sex, were the ingredients that made up much of the fiction centred on the train, and the same elements featured in what was certainly the best film on the subject, Alfred Hitchcock's *The Lady Vanishes* (1938). Not everyone, however, approved of the high life of the train, and D.H. Lawrence expressed his rather puritanical views through, of all characters, Constance, Lady Chatterley: 'He took berths on the Orient Express, in spite of Connie's dislike of trains de luxe, the atmosphere of vulgar depravity there is aboard them nowadays.' High adventure or vulgar depravity – the readers could decide for themselves. But what was the reality? In 1935, a new partwork began publication in Britain, *Railway Wonders of the World*. One issue contained a first-hand account of a journey on the Orient Express, starting in London and proceeding via Constanta to Istanbul. Though bereft of spies and temptresses, it boasts a wealth of technical detail.

The first part of the journey begins on the Continental Express that set off from London at 2.00 p.m. for the ferry to Calais. There, the writer was a little disappointed to find just

LEFT *It took over thirty years for Agatha Christie's novel* Murder on the Orient Express *to reach the screen. It was eventually filmed in 1974, with Albert Finney as Hercule Poirot.*

one of the famous royal blue coaches, and that was attached to the end of a very ordinary Nord express train. At 5.25 p.m., however, they were under way to connect with the Simplon-Orient, which would be leaving the Gare de l'Est some two and a half hours later. The journey remained uneventful as the train sped across northern France to Châlons, where the Nord express slipped its solitary Wagons-Lits coach, which was then attached to the waiting Simplon. Where he had previously been unimpressed, the anonymous writer was now all enthusiasm. He wrote in glowing terms of the opulence of the carriages and the smooth running of the train, a credit to the rolling stock and to the newly improved permanent way. If there is still a slight hint of disappointment, it is only because the train was headed by one of the big 4-6-2 Pacific-type French locomotives, and not by one of the even more imposing 4-8-2 Mountain class.

By now, most passengers had retired and the conductors had collected up tickets and passports to cope with border formalities while everyone else slept – except our eager writer. He was able to report on the first change of locomotives at Strasbourg, where a German engine replaced the French, and he was still alert at 4.32 a.m. when the train arrived at Karlsruhe, where there was another change, this time to a splendid Pacific of the Baden State Railway. He remained awake when Stuttgart was reached just after 6.00 a.m., for this was to offer something very new. Steam now gave way to electricity, with a big twelve-wheel engine taking power

BELOW *The Orient Express circa 1928. Immense locomotives were being introduced onto French railways, but here a more modest 310 class engine seems perfectly adequate.*

from overhead lines carrying 15,000 volts. Although obviously a man in love with the romance of steam, he could not deny the superior efficiency of the electric locomotive. He described the journey across the mountains: 'Until recently, the negotiation of this section used to be accompanied by much laboured puffing, which – with heavy trains containing three classes of coach – came from behind as well as in front. Now the big electric glides up the incline almost silently, and when she reaches the down grade beyond the summit, she glides down it in the same imperturbable fashion. The old steam engines used to sprint down as if they were frantically making up for the previous up-hill crawl.'

There is no need to follow him every mile of the way, through every change of engine, for none went unremarked upon, as he noted with interest the taper boiler on the Austrian 2-4-0 with its bulbous, spark-arrester chimney, and deplored finding the world's ugliest locomotives in Hungary. He noted how the train dashed through France, covering the 112 miles (180 km) from Châlons to Nancy in just two hours, but gradually slowed as it moved east until, by the

ABOVE *Iselle station at the Italian end of the Simplon tunnel. By 1921, though steam was still in use for the train de luxe, an electric locomotive can be seen on the left of the picture.*

time it was into the Balkans, it was reduced to 'a sort of loping trot, dignified but uninspiring'. It had all been a great experience, but the writer could not help noting that, splendid as the Orient Express undoubtedly was, it was still run on a railway philosophy developed in the nineteenth century, and the railway world was changing fast. Mitropa was now offering a serious challenge to all other luxury trains, by providing second-class compartments with sleeping berths. These trains were as comfortable, if not as grand, as the Orient Express and a good deal cheaper. The Orient had no choice, and in the latter years of the 1930s, it too began to offer second-class sleepers, with two berths per compartment instead of one. It seemed positively revolutionary to Wagons-Lits, but far greater, cataclysmic changes were to occur in the very near future.

Its travelling days may be over, but this car, rather than being turned into just another museum exhibit, has found a new role as a cafe.

CHAPTER FIVE

The End of the Line

The emergence of Hitler and the National Socialists in Germany did not have an immediate effect on the international scene, at least as far as the limited interests of railway companies was concerned. Although in 1934, the German parliament had voluntarily signed away its own rights and given Hitler virtually unlimited powers, all his efforts at first were concentrated on internal affairs. But once he had eliminated all opposition and felt his position completely assured, he turned to other matters. 1938 was the year of the Anschluss, when he marched into Austria and took over the country in a bloodless coup. This certainly was of concern to the railway world, for Germany also took control of Austria's railways and promptly tore up all the contracts negotiated with Wagons-Lits.

As German expansionism moved remorselessly eastward, the world at last woke up to what was happening, but much too late. With the invasion of Poland in 1939, Britain and France declared war on Germany. Then came a curious lull, when everyone seemed to be holding their breath, the months of the 'phoney war'. Incredible as it seems, the Simplon-Orient Express continued running its luxury trains as if nothing of any great importance had happened, even accepting connections from Berlin. Sections of the Arlberg-Orient also still continued to function, though only because most of the route was already firmly under German control. With the Fall of France in June 1940, all pretences of normality were finally dropped.

ABOVE *Some carriages that had been used by the German army were later taken over by the victorious American forces, and given the official badge of the U.S. Army Transportation Corps.*

RIGHT *During World War II, throughout Europe, the German Army used many Wagons-Lits carriages for anything from officers' quarters to brothels. Afterwards, Wagons-Lits had the difficult job of retrieving them for renovation.*

Everyone knew that an era had ended, but the Orient Express had not yet vanished from the world stage and still had some starring roles to play. The first was in a drama that harked back to the days of endless intrigues between the Balkan states. As a result of the Russo–German non-aggression pact, signed just before the rest of Europe tumbled into war, these two great powers agreed not to fight each other. They now felt free to pounce as predators on the smaller prey. They began the plunder of Romania. King Carol showed no desire to be a martyr for his country: his only concern was to get out, with his deeply unpopular mistress, Magda Lupescu, taking as much loot as they could with them. On 8 September, two Wagons-Lits salons and a sleeping car were shunted into Bucharest station. A version of the Orient Express was still making a curtailed journey through central Europe, but for Carol there was only one place of interest, neutral Switzerland, with its accommodating and discreet bankers. The couple joined the train, accompanied by a large truck full of valuables, removed from the palace, national treasures ranging from old master paintings to precious jewels, which Carol simply appropriated as though they were his personal property. Their suitcases were crammed full of foreign currency, mostly Swiss francs and American dollars. The three-coach train set off on the journey, with the king and Magda cowering in one compartment, heading for exile. The couple ended their days in a luxurious villa in Portugal. It was not one of the more elevating episodes in the history of the Orient Express.

By 1942, the Orient Express was still running a limited service, through German-occupied territory and under German control. The days of travelling purely for pleasure were over, however. Only those who had to do so travelled on the railways at all, for they were the most popular target for resistance fighters, particularly in France and Greece. The Orient Express had become, in all but name, a military train, but some concessions were made to its former existence, when permission was granted to certain foreign diplomats to use the service. This concession gave rise to another dramatic journey, in total contrast with King Carol's scuttle to affluent safety. An eminent Swedish banker, Raoul Wallenberg, was persuaded to go on a mission of mercy in 1944, in an attempt to save the surviving Jews in Hungary. He was given papers authorising him to travel to take up a post at the neutral Swedish embassy in Berlin, under whose auspices he would then continue his journey east. Funds for the rescue mission were provided by the American government, and Mr Wallenberg's luggage was a mass of secret compartments, each stuffed with banknotes. Eventually reaching Budapest, he used the money to buy fake papers, enabling thousands of

Jews to escape death. Sadly, having survived the Nazis, he died in a KGB prison, allegedly of a heart attack.

RESISTANCE

It was a matter of pride to the Germans to be able to claim that they could run the famous train through the war years, in spite of the regular attacks by saboteurs. They attempted to portray the resistance fighters as terrorists who showed no mercy for the ordinary citizens who used the railways. Posters were printed in France, offering a reward of a million francs to anyone giving information that led to the arrest of resistance fighters. The old Wagons-Lits staff who had continued to serve on the trains had to face a terrible dilemma. Everything in their lives had been centred around the idea that their first duty was always to the train and its passengers, yet many of them took immense risks in helping the resistance to destroy the trains they loved. Some paid the penalty. In all, seven Orient Express conductors were executed by firing squad, and many more were sent to concentration camps in Germany. This is a great testimony to the patriotism of these men, for with the service reduced to a minimum, only a few staff were kept on. The proportion of those prepared to make the sacrifice must have been very high. The cars that were no longer in service found other uses. Many sleeping cars provided luxury accommodation for German officers and officials in the occupied territories, while a few suffered the indignity of being converted into military brothels.

As the fortunes of war changed following the D-Day landings of June 1944, the carriages that had once served the German occupying forces were abandoned, and now they served the commanders of the army of liberation. In May 1945, the war in Europe came to an end, and the long task of restoring devastated countries and their economies began. For Wagons-Lits, it meant rebuilding a rail network across Europe all over again. On 27 September of that year, the Arlberg Express once again drew away from the Gare de l'Est with an invited party of dignitaries from Wagons-Lits, the French national railway (SNCF) and French Army officers on board. At the border, they were joined by railway officals from Switzerland and on it went, past stations hung with flags and bunting, to its destination at Innsbruck, where even more flags flew and the band played a rousing welcome. It was not exactly the Arlberg-Orient Express of old, but it was a start on the road back to normality.

It was an extraordinary achievement to get this far in a Europe that had been ravaged, its cities destroyed and its economic life reduced to a near shambles. There were far more people whose only concern was to get enough food to eat than there were businessmen and wealthy dilettantes looking to enjoy the luxuries of first-class travel. It was, however, very important to show confidence in the future, and ensure that as things did get better, so the services would be ready and waiting. The greatest problem for the company in the first years after World War II was the same as it had been after World War I – collecting together and patching up whatever rolling stock could be found. Search parties set out to find Wagons-Lits cars, sometimes barely recognisable under wartime camouflage. When, at the end of the exercise, inventories were drawn up, it was found that 189 coaches were missing, presumably destroyed in the fighting, 110 were so old and battered as not to be worth saving, and 200 were damaged but repairable. There was an obvious, and urgent, need to build new coaches and no time to think about fundamental design changes to make them appropriate for a new age. There had to be some changes, however. The YT class, for example, was almost shockingly new, in that there were first-, second- and third-class compartments all in the same coach, with one, two and three berths respectively. Thirty of these were put into production in the late 1940s. At the opposite end of the scale, the luxury LX class was still being built, intended mainly for use on the Orient Express. With the future shape of the European rail network still uncertain, it was also prudent to assume that there would be an increased demand for comfortable day coaches, and a new Pullman building programme was put in hand as well. Building and renewing coaches was only a part of the problem. Crockery, cutlery, glasses and linen all needed replacing if anything like the old standards were to be reclaimed.

A TIME OF RENEWAL

The problems of renewal, though manageable, were immense, and made far worse by the shortage of raw materials and damaged factories and machinery. The problems created by international politics were a very different matter. The final assault on Germany had taken place on two fronts, the Russians advancing from the East and the western Allies fighting their way up through France from the Normandy beaches. At the peace, this division became fixed into areas of influence. Europe was divided into two mutually distrustful and increasingly hostile power blocs. The Soviet Union, in particular, showed a single-minded ruthlessness in imposing its will on the occupied territories. Communist control over eastern Europe was absolute: the Cold War had begun.

The political changes did not happen at once, and there was a period immediately after the war when the two sides were

RIGHT *The Simplon-Orient Express waits at the little station of Uzunköprü in Turkey. There is a timeless quality about the scene, and the sleeping car that has stopped here in 1950 looks out on a vista that would have been much the same in the 1930s.*

prepared to co-operate in allowing the smooth running of a railway system that criss-crossed the different zones of influence. At first, the process was helped by the fact that the two sides had a mutual interest in hunting for war criminals, for whom international trains offered the best hope of escape to a safe haven. That situation, however, soon began to change when escapees on the run were no longer a small number of former Nazis, but a flood of refugees from the communist regimes. Some were wealthy and anxious to take whatever they could of their valuables with them. Border controls became a nightmare as officials searched for illegal emigrants, smugglers and, that old stalwart of the Orient Express, spies. In a world of acute shortages,

there were fortunes to be made on the black market from all kinds of commodities, from pharmaceuticals to gold bars. The international train was still the favoured method of moving many valuables, particularly if the train staff could be bribed to help with concealment. And if the staff continued to uphold the old Wagons-Lits tradition of scrupulous honesty, one could always turn to the far more bribable border guards themselves.

Life was becoming increasingly difficult for Wagons-Lits. The new authorities in Hungary and Romania were ideologically opposed to the whole concept of a luxury train, and insisted that, although the sleeping cars and dining cars would be allowed to run, they could not make up a whole train:

they must also be accompanied by more democratic coaches, offering second- and third-class accommodation. The old Orient Express could no longer advertise itself as a luxury train. The Arlberg-Orient was not under the same constraints, but even here a second-class Pullman coach was added, which proved very popular, offering a good deal more comfort than was usually found in that class. If the word 'luxury' was being eased out of the railway vocabulary, so too the word 'Express' had little meaning for much of the service. It was not that speeds along the rails had been reduced, but that the interminable stops at frontiers were making nonsense of the printed timetables. Searches had to be made and papers

ABOVE *This 1950s photograph has something of the glum austerity of post-war years. The first-class carriage, with its old-fashioned radiator and footrest, now seems rather spartan.*

siding. Then there would be more searches, and every single passenger would be subjected to prolonged interrogation.

There was an ever-present frisson of danger about travel in those days as the train passed from one control zone to another. Stops could seem sinister and unnerving to even the most innocent of passengers. Borders were as likely to be in the middle of the country as at a station, with its reassuring crowds of ordinary citizens, and could take place at any time of day or night. The train would come to a halt, and at night the passengers would awaken unsure of just where they were. All that would be apparent would be the police and soldiers, suspicious and belligerent, emerging from the darkness. This was just the situation that confronted two American travellers, Lucille Vogeler and her sister, en route to a skiing holiday in the Austrian Tyrol. The border between the American and Soviet Zones was the River Inn, some miles from Innsbruck. The women had their passports and papers of authorisation, allowing them to pass through the Soviet zone, but the guard brusquely informed them that everything was certainly not in order. They were forced to get dressed and leave the train. The conductor collected their bags and set them down beside them, then climbed back on board, and the train started off again. Aghast, they saw its lights disappear into the night and heard the steady beat of the engine fade away into silence. They were alone in a hostile country with interrogators who refused their request for a call to the American high commissioner in Vienna. At last, a Russian officer appeared to authorise their release, but there was to be no skiing holiday. Instead, they were ordered onto the next train to Vienna, with clear instructions never to appear in the Soviet zone again. But these were not – it soon transpired – quite the arbitrary proceedings they had at first seemed.

THE THIRD MAN

Lucille Vogeler's husband, Robert, had made regular use of the Orient Express to visit Budapest and Prague, and the authorities in the East were convinced that his visits had less to do with his legitimate business as a telecommunications executive than with illicit communications of a different kind. In spite of the treatment his wife had received, he continued to visit the East, and, in February 1950, he and a Briton, Edgar Sanders, were arrested in Hungary and charged with spying. He was found guilty and sentenced to fifteen years in prison, but thanks to back-stage diplomacy he was released in just over a year, and Sanders was freed in 1953. The Hungarians were sure there was a third man involved with them, a U.S. naval attaché in Bucharest, Captain Eugene Karp. On the arrest of the other two men, Karp was at once recalled to Washington – a move that merely confirmed Hungarian suspicions. He left aboard the Arlberg-Orient Express bound for Paris, but never arrived. The

examined, and it was a rare day indeed when all papers were found to be in order. Many passengers discovered that the 'correct' papers could often be found in their wallets. It was very frustrating, but just about manageable.

Routes became dependent on politics more than convenience. In 1947, a conference was held in Istanbul to decide how the connections between the Balkans and western Europe could be maintained. The Arlberg-Orient Express was extended to Bucharest, and a brand new service authorised, called the Balt-Orient Express, which provided a sleeping car service from Oslo to Prague and from Stockholm to Belgrade. Meanwhile the Orient Express was enjoying a far from happy return to service. The authorities in eastern Europe who had already insisted that it could no longer run as a *train de luxe*, were becoming increasingly suspicious. Searches became longer and more thorough, and the discovery of smuggled goods or currency anywhere on the train would result not just in arrests and confiscation, but in the whole train being shunted into a attendant in his sleeping car was drugged, and Karp's compartment had not been slept in. His body was found in the Lüg tunnel, and the story was put out by local officials that he must have been drunk, inadvertently opened the wrong door and fallen out of the train. No one explained how he had closed the door after himself. Investigators, however, found traces of blood on the tunnel wall; and tests, using sandbags to simulate a heavy body, showed that for stains to appear in such a place Karp must have been violently hurled from the train by at least two strong men. No one had any doubt that the third man had not been allowed to escape to the West. This was a real and brutal murder on the Orient Express, not a work of fiction.

MISERY

It must sometimes have seemed to the harassed staff at Wagons-Lits that the main objective of international diplomacy was to make their lives a misery. No sooner had a new route been opened than some fresh obstacle appeared, and the search was on for yet another alternative. In 1949, Czechoslovakia and Hungary, which had already shown their distaste for what they saw as the capitalist decadence of the Orient Express, officially withdrew all running rights. Relations between the western powers and Yugoslavia were, however, improving as the country's leader Tito distanced

himself from Moscow, while at the same time accepting a massive loan from America; and the civil war in Greece had come to an end. This meant that there was a way open for the Simplon-Orient Express to run through Yugoslavia, Greece, Macedonia and Bulgaria into Turkey. So, for 1949 at least, the good news and the bad news seemed to cancel each other out. But, preoccupied as they were with their international juggling act, the railway planners did not perhaps appreciate the significance of an event that took place on 27 July of that year. In Britain, the De Havilland Company announced the maiden flight of a brand new type of aircraft, the Comet jet airliner. Sixteen of these planes had already been ordered, and were expected to go into service in 1952. It did not pose an immediate threat to rail travel, but it would not be many years before passengers came to see a flight of a few hours as being preferable to a train journey lasting days.

Then, just as everything seemed to have settled down on the international scene, Turkey quarrelled with Bulgaria and the frontier between them was closed. As a result, trains either had to stop in Sofia or occasionally trundle on to Svilengrad, where

BELOW *With the post-war years came the construction of coaches with bodies of aluminium instead of steel, which looked more North American than European.*

passengers could, tantalisingly, peer across the border into Turkey. The disagreement was soon settled, but then Greece and Bulgaria disagreed, and closed that border. This meant an even more serious curtailment of rail services, and the Orient Express would have stopped well short of its oriental destination, if there had not been yet another policy reverse. This time, Turkey and Greece decided to make up and re-open the border. The new route went through Salonica (Thessaloníki) and Thrace to Istanbul. If the reader is now feeling a little confused by all these changes, just imagine the headaches endured by headquarters staff as they tried to piece routes together, not to mention the long-suffering passenger trying to sort out the timetables. Even Mother Nature, on occasion, added to the confusion. In 1951, floods in northern Italy closed the Simplon tunnel, and the trains had to be rerouted through the Mont Cenis tunnel.

THE NAME'S BOND

By the early 1950s, something like stability seemed to have been established at last, but no one could pretend that life had returned to normal. The early runs through Greece to Turkey were fraught with danger, for although the war was officially over, there were still armed bands of guerrillas in the hills, and a luxury train was a tempting target. No one took that ride unless they were on essential business, and even then the train only ran over the most dangerous sections in daylight and with an armed escort. This was the route chosen by Ian Fleming in *From Russia with Love* (1955) for James Bond's near fatal encounter with an agent of that most evil of all fictional organisations, SMERSH. The fight on the train could easily have been inspired by the tragic death of Captain Karp, though no one really expected the fictional super-hero to suffer the same fate as the real naval attaché. Fleming, always a romantic, was clearly an admirer of the train and all it stood for: 'The great trains are going out all over Europe, but still, three times a week, the Orient Express thunders superbly over 1400 miles of glittering steel track between Istanbul and Paris.' The situation eventually became calmer, but it was not a propitious start for a service struggling to re-establish itself after the war years.

As old members of the Orient Express family were retired, so newcomers arrived to take their place. Of these the most spectacular was the Tauern-Orient Express, which ran from Ostend to Athens. It took its name from the Hohe Tauern mountain range in Austria, which rises to a height of 12,457 feet (3797 metres). The Tauern line, built in the 1930s, was one of the great engineering achievements of the age, involving the construction of nearly 10 miles (16 km) of tunnels through the mountains as part of a line which had a total length of just 50 miles (80 km). The route begins by climbing up the beautiful Gasteiner Valley towards Badgastein at a height of 3550 feet (1082 metres), one of the most picturesque towns in the region, with a mighty waterfall rushing down through the centre of the town. Passengers had to make the most of the mountain views, for soon they would be entering the first of seventeen tunnels through the mountains and, sadly, from the point of view of sightseeing, the summit of the line at 4022 feet (1226 metres) is right in the middle of the Tauern tunnel itself. The final section of the rail link leads down towards Mallnitz, close to the Yugoslav border. The journey itself was not as arduous as one might have expected, for it was fully electrified as early as 1935. Another new line, the Balkan Express, took a great swing round the forbidden territories of Hungary and Bulgaria to link Vienna to Belgrade and Athens, and was extended by 1955 to Sofia and Istanbul.

All this was a long way from Nagelmackers' original dream of an express train made up of the most comfortable railway carriages ever built, thundering on a direct route across Europe to Turkey and the East. Now routes were determined by politics not geography, and the standards that had to be accepted in the second half of the twentieth century fell a long way short of those of the early years. The problems were not of Wagons-Lits' making, and it did its best to preserve traditions while keeping up with modern trends. One of its greatest assets had always been the train crews, and here, at least, standards were still high, and the company made sure that they looked the part. New uniforms were introduced in 1949. A *chef de train* was given the type of uniform that would have been happily worn by an army general, topped by a cap with an oak-leaf motif on the peak – and to add to the military appearance, lesser ranks were expected to salute him. The waiters now sported ties and waistcoats, though the conductors still retained the high collar of an earlier age, as if to reassure the passengers that some things at least remained unchanged. They and the waiters were also awarded chevrons, one for every five years' service with the company. The cleaners were issued with blouses, giving them the vague air of peasant farmers who had somehow strayed into a railway station. But nothing could disguise the fact that things had changed, and changed radically.

BELOW *By the 1960s, as this poster shows, the stylishness that had defined Wagons-Lits for almost a century was fast fading.*

BELOW *This 1958 photograph of a sleeping car clearly shows the brilliant, bold Art Deco motifs designed by René Prou.*

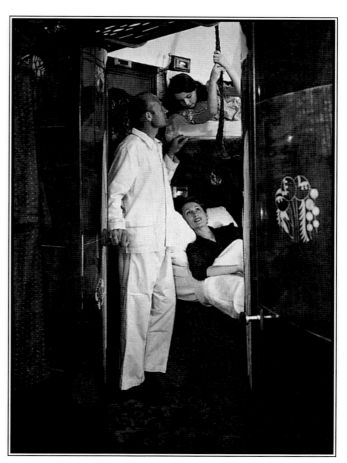

ABOVE *In an attempt to economise, second-class compartments were introduced onto the Orient Express for the first time.*

RIGHT *Another 1950s publicity photograph showing some obvious changes from the past.*

Wagons-Lits cars were attached to any train that wanted them, but it did at least ensure that passengers could still get into a carriage and stay in it all the way to Istanbul. It was known as the Direct Orient, and it offered through carriages, but not a through train. At best there would be a couple of sleeping cars, and, on good days, a restaurant car, and these were almost lost in trains made up of assorted carriages from many countries and covering every class of compartment. If there was still a demand for luxury travel, it was not a very important factor in the Balkan countries, so that the Wagons-Lits coaches were no longer considered the most important part of the train as a whole. Most travellers ignored them altogether, treating the train just like any other local express, staying with it for perhaps no more than a couple of stops. Inevitably, this made life increasingly difficult for the Direct Orient. As more ordinary coaches were added, so it looked less and less like a luxury train, and its appeal diminished. The operating companies in the different countries saw that this was so, appreciated the increased demand for purely local services, and made that their priority. More ordinary coaches were added, more stops cluttered the timetable. Every change made the train less appealing to the rich, and the decline accelerated.

THE JET SET

It might have been possible to maintain the service had other things been equal, but they were not. In an earlier age, passengers had been attracted by the very idea of the Orient Express and its air of romantic exoticism combined with comforting notions of service and luxury. At the same time, a very high proportion of the passengers used the train because they needed to travel. The train offered the quickest, most comfortable route to the East, and they were prepared to pay extra for the privileges. Now, things were different. The immediate threat to train travel posed by the Comet airliner had not materialised. After just two years, and a series of fatal accidents, the plane had been withdrawn from service. But that did not stop the inexorable advance of the airliner. As early as 1956, British European Airways were offering cheap, non-stop flights from London to Paris, Milan and Zurich. The arrival of the Boeing 707 confirmed that a new age of travel really had begun. Why spend days crossing Europe in a train hauled by that marvel of nineteenth-century technology, the steam locomotive, when the same journey could be made in hours by jet airliner? True, there were no four- and five-course dinners, no fine wines, no comfortable compartments with a conductor always on call, but who needed them when a flight could take off after lunch and arrive at the destination in time for dinner? The journey was no longer something that was there to be enjoyed for its own sake, it was simply the quickest route

The Arlberg-Orient Express managed to retain one sleeping car on the run to Bucharest, but in May 1962 even that was removed. Now the train went no further than Vienna, and as no one could pretend that the capital of Austria had anything oriental in its character, the Arlberg-Orient became plain Arlberg Express. A few days later, a similar fate overtook the other famous line, which also had its title reduced, becoming the Simplon Express. Did this mark the end of the Orient Express? In a sense it did, but a service of sorts still struggled on between Paris and Istanbul, using Wagons-Lits cars. It was rather like a return to the earliest days of the company, when the

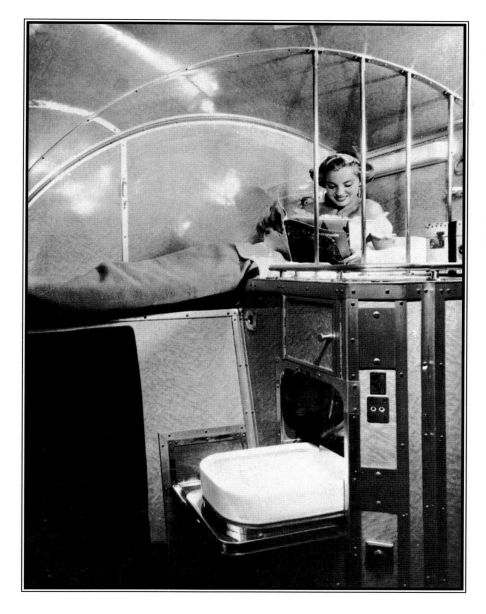

ABOVE *The end of the line: the departure board for the very last Direct Orient to leave Paris for Istanbul. Scheduled to leave at 11.56 p.m. on 19 May 1977, the clocks ticked past midnight before it finally left the station – a day late.*

LEFT *In the 1960s, Wagons-Lits made a complete break with tradition, with the emphasis on function and simplicity. In this sleeping compartment, the retractable wash-basin has been pulled out for use; this could be stowed away later. The curved rails by the bunk are very much of the period, even if the effect seems disconcertingly like the bars of a cell.*

between two points. If that was now the main criterion, then there was little chance of long-distance rail travel competing with the airlines.

Still, the Orient Express battled on. In 1964, the route was extended from Vienna by the Vienna-Budapest Express, and the following year a limited sleeping car service was run to Bucharest. The Simplon Express divided at Milan, one part going to Venice and Trieste as in the old days, the other to Florence, Rome and Naples. There were to be more route shuffles over the years, and more renamings; even an extension over a much-improved Yugoslav permanent way to Belgrade. Even if travel times were not comparable to the airlines', one could leave Paris in the early evening, enjoy a gourmet dinner, retire for the night and wake up to the glories of Venice – and all without the longueurs of airport departure lounges and check-in queues.

THE LAST FAREWELL

The last years of the Orient Express were like the sad decline of an old friend: everyone knew death was inevitable, but no one was quite sure when the end would come. The Direct Orient, the last of the line to carry the magic word in the title, actually began running again in 1969. It set out from Calais with a single YU-class sleeper, a survivor from more spacious days. The original Y class, with twenty-one berths, was already quite crowded by Wagons-Lits standards, but this had now been extended to thirty. It was joined by two composite coaches, with first- and second-class compartments. At Nis, the train divided into the Athens Express and the Marmara Express, which took the seaside route into Istanbul. It must have been a logistical nightmare, bringing all the different elements together, with different coaches and different locomotives for different countries and regions. First there were the locomotives – twelve in all on the Istanbul run

LEFT *Just before the 1977 auction of rolling stock, there was a farewell run from Nice to Monte Carlo. Among the guests was Princess Grace of Monaco, seen here in Pullman restaurant car No. 4163, which was eventually bought by the King of Morocco.*

from Paris, ten to Athens. These included four different types of electric locomotives, each working with a different current and voltage, the new generation of diesels and just the occasional puff of steam. Coaches came and went, it seemed, at every stop. Not surprisingly, journey times as set out in the timetable indicated a slow trudge across Europe, at an average speed for the whole journey of a niggardly 33 mph (54 kph). It was all rather like joining an 1800 mile (2896 km) long traffic jam.

There was no longer even any pretence of attracting the old style of wealthy passenger. In time, even the dining car was sacrificed, and the best that anyone could expect was a hurriedly grabbed snack at a buffet or a plastic tray of apparently plastic food, of the kind already proving all too familiar on international airlines. The wise took their own provisions.

Fewer and fewer tickets were sold for the entire journey, and as a result fewer berths were reserved in the sleeping cars. Wagons-Lits was already coming to terms with the inevitable. In 1974, Thomas Cook announced that it would no longer be offering continental sleeping car bookings at its European offices. Even the company name changed, in a sad admission that the glory days really were over. The Compagnie Internationale des Wagons-Lits et des Grands Express Européens became Compagnie Internationale des Wagons-Lits et du Tourisme, the name change reflecting the group's diversification into new activities, including travel agency services, hotels and catering.

It was a slow death, but in 1977 the announcement was finally made. The last through train would depart for Istanbul, on 19 May and leave for the return to Paris on the 22nd. It was perhaps all too typical of the last years that it was late. Scheduled to depart at 11.56 p.m., it actually pulled away from the platform at 0.13 a.m.: a day's reprieve, for it was now the 20th. Having been ignored for years, the old train was now the centre of excited attention. The train was packed, crowds jammed the platform, cameras clicked and whirred, anybody who could be interviewed was interviewed. Some maintained that this was not really the end, for the Arlberg and Simplon Expresses were still running, but they were not the Orient Express. It really was the end – or so it seemed.

In October 1977, there was an auction of Wagons-Lits rolling stock at Monte Carlo. Now that the trains no longer ran, the old cars had been recognised for the splendid things that they were. Purchasers included the King of Morocco and, more significantly for the future, James Sherwood of Sea Containers Ltd. The crowds that had gathered to see the last run hinted at a brand new market, based not on the need to get from place to place, but on a very powerful sentiment – nostalgia. It might not be possible to sell train tickets to people rushing to a business meeting on the far side of the continent, but a virtue could be made of a gentler pace,

offering a return to a more gracious age. The plan was to bring back all the luxury, the sumptuous fare, the personal attention and the sybaritic comforts of the past – and charge accordingly. The train would no longer be a means to an end – it was itself the main attraction. The Orient Express was to be reborn as an old fashioned *train de luxe*, and it was to prove a huge success, but it was a different creature. Throughout its working life, the aim had been to make the Orient Express the best, the most modern and most efficient train in Europe. The new train was a deliberate step back into the past. It was part of a new luxury travel trade that aimed to recreate the past – travelling on a former maharajah's train through India or steaming across the Trans-Siberian Railway. The true Orient Express, the train that had its fixed place in the timetables of Europe, came to an end in 1977. There has never been a train that gripped the popular imagination as the Orient Express did, none that ever had the same piquant air of romance. There has never been a train that crossed so many frontiers, from the plains to the mountains, all the time wrapping its charges in a cocoon of pampered comfort. And we are unlikely ever to see one again. The Orient Express was, is and will remain, unique.

RIGHT *Car No. 3489, built at the Metro works in Britain in 1929 and featuring flower basket marquetry by Morison. It was one of the historic coaches sold by Sotheby's at an auction in Monaco in October 1977.*

BELOW *Film star Ingrid Bergman is lulled into a state of relaxed dreaminess by Wagons-Lits' fabled luxury.*

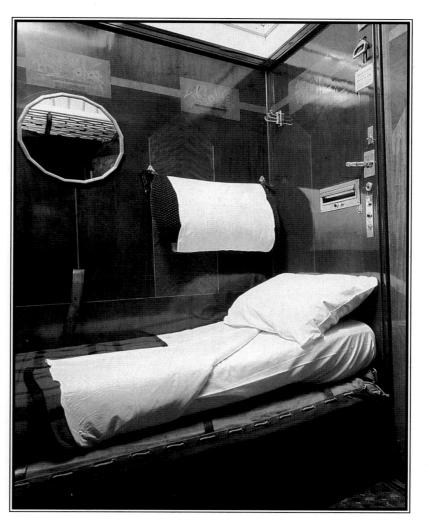

Carriages in Use

HISTORY OF THE CARRIAGES

A great part of the appeal of the Orient Express lies in the fact that Wagons-Lits was responsible for the manufacture of some of the most splendid carriages ever built. One can view these cars in museums, but to appreciate them to the full, one should really see them on the move and, best of all, travel in them.

NENE VALLEY RAILWAY

Unlike most British preserved railways, Cambridgeshire's Nene Valley has a distinctly European air. Alongside famous British locomotives are engines from Sweden, Denmark, Germany, Italy and France, while the carriages include two Wagons-Lits coaches.

CAR NO. 2975

Built in 1927 by Officine Meccaniche Italiane at Reggio-Emilia, Italy, this was one of 75 standard dining cars of the period, each built for 56 diners. It had a very mixed career, starting service in Italy, moving on to Paris, Vienna and Basle, and remaining in Switzerland throughout the war. After a refit in 1963, the carriage was used on the Simplon Express and other routes before being withdrawn in 1977. It was bought by Thomas Cook in 1978 to celebrate the company's 50-year association with Wagons-Lits, and was presented on long-term loan to the Nene Valley Railway.

CAR NO. 3916

This YT class sleeping car of 1949 is currently in very poor condition, and languishing in a siding.

THE VENICE-SIMPLON-ORIENT EXPRESS

The service had its origins in the Monte Carlo sale of old Wagons-Lits carriages, two of which were purchased by James B. Sherwood, with a view to restoring the glories of the Orient Express. On 25 May 1982, passengers again gathered for the train for Venice. They began their journey in traditional brown and cream Pullman coaches, but once over the Channel they were transferred to the famous royal blue of Wagons-Lits. Further services were added, and to celebrate the millennium a through train ran once more from Paris to Istanbul.

CAR NO. 3309

Built by Les Ateliers de Construction Métallurgique in Belgium in 1926, this is one of the first all-steel S class coaches. A notable feature of this carriage is the Art Deco marquetry designed by René Prou, with highly stylised plant motifs. The car was used on various Orient Express routes from 1929 to 1939, and was involved in the famous freezing winter of that first year. Fortunately for the passengers, it was not left stranded in the wilderness, but came to a halt at the station of Alpullu in the Turkish mountains. The carriage later worked in Germany from 1942 to 1945. after which it was tracked down by Wagons-Lits and put back on the Orient Express. In 1958, it was sent to Portugal, and the interior was modified to take 24 passengers instead of the original 16. It was withdrawn from service in 1971.

CAR NO. 3425

Also with designs by Prou, this car was built by the Birmingham Railway Carriage and Wagon Company in 1929. Shipped out on the continental train ferry from Harwich to Zeebrugge, it had a varied career on the Orient Express network and on the Engadine Oberland Express, connecting Paris to the fashionable ski resort of St Moritz. At the outbreak of war, the car was back on the Simplon-Orient Express and was one of the carriages attached to the train in which King Carol of Romania and Magda Lupescu fled to exile. In 1940, the car was sent to Turkey, and ended the first stage of its working life in Portugal.

CAR NO. 3473

Built by Metropolitan Cammell in Birmingham, this car has marquetry by the English designer Morison, in a conventional 'flower garland' pattern, with bunches of flowers contained in a border of stylised swags. The carriage ran on the Blue Train until 1937, when it joined the Nord Express, running from Paris to the Russian border. It remained in Paris during the war, and was restored to the Blue Train in 1946. After being transferred to the Simplon in 1961, it was taken out of service in 1971.

CAR NO. 3482

This car, like No. 3473, was built by Metropolitan Cammell, but differs in that the marquetry was designed by Maple and executed by Albert Dunn, whose son was responsible for its restoration. The 'Trapeze' design shows a strong Cubist influence and fits well with the Art Deco look of features such as the metal luggage racks. The car ran on the BlueTrain and the Nord Express. During the war years it served as a temporary hotel in Lyon. After the war, it ran on the Blue Train and the Lombardy and Simplon Expresses. It also ran in Spain from 1969 to 1971.

perhaps all too typical of the last years that it was late. Scheduled to depart at 11.56 p.m., it actually pulled away from the platform at 0.13 a.m.: a day's reprieve, for it was now the 20th. Having been ignored for years, the old train was now the centre of excited attention. The train was packed, crowds jammed the platform, cameras clicked and whirred, anybody who could be interviewed was interviewed. Some maintained that this was not really the end, for the Arlberg and Simplon Expresses were still running, but they were not the Orient Express. It really was the end – or so it seemed.

In October 1977, there was an auction of Wagons-Lits rolling stock at Monte Carlo. Now that the trains no longer ran, the old cars had been recognised for the splendid things that they were. Purchasers included the King of Morocco and, more significantly for the future, James Sherwood of Sea Containers Ltd. The crowds that had gathered to see the last run hinted at a brand new market, based not on the need to get from place to place, but on a very powerful sentiment – nostalgia. It might not be possible to sell train tickets to people rushing to a business meeting on the far side of the continent, but a virtue could be made of a gentler pace, offering a return to a more gracious age. The plan was to bring back all the luxury, the sumptuous fare, the personal attention and the sybaritic comforts of the past – and charge accordingly. The train would no longer be a means to an end – it was itself the main attraction. The Orient Express was to be reborn as an old fashioned *train de luxe*, and it was to prove a huge success, but it was a different creature. Throughout its working life, the aim had been to make the Orient Express the best, the most modern and most efficient train in Europe. The new train was a deliberate step back into the past. It was part of a new luxury travel trade that aimed to recreate the past – travelling on a former maharajah's train through India or steaming across the Trans-Siberian Railway. The true Orient Express, the train that had its fixed place in the timetables of Europe, came to an end in 1977. There has never been a train that gripped the popular imagination as the Orient Express did, none that ever had the same piquant air of romance. There has never been a train that crossed so many frontiers, from the plains to the mountains, all the time wrapping its charges in a cocoon of pampered comfort. And we are unlikely ever to see one again. The Orient Express was, is and will remain, unique.

RIGHT *Car No. 3489, built at the Metro works in Britain in 1929 and featuring flower basket marquetry by Morison. It was one of the historic coaches sold by Sotheby's at an auction in Monaco in October 1977.*

BELOW *Film star Ingrid Bergman is lulled into a state of relaxed dreaminess by Wagons-Lits' fabled luxury.*

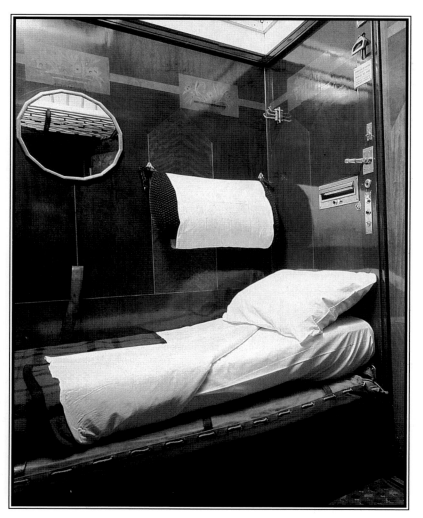

Carriages in Use

HISTORY OF THE CARRIAGES

A great part of the appeal of the Orient Express lies in the fact that Wagons-Lits was responsible for the manufacture of some of the most splendid carriages ever built. One can view these cars in museums, but to appreciate them to the full, one should really see them on the move and, best of all, travel in them.

NENE VALLEY RAILWAY

Unlike most British preserved railways, Cambridgeshire's Nene Valley has a distinctly European air. Alongside famous British locomotives are engines from Sweden, Denmark, Germany, Italy and France, while the carriages include two Wagons-Lits coaches.

CAR No. 2975

Built in 1927 by Officine Meccaniche Italiane at Reggio-Emilia, Italy, this was one of 75 standard dining cars of the period, each built for 56 diners. It had a very mixed career, starting service in Italy, moving on to Paris, Vienna and Basle, and remaining in Switzerland throughout the war. After a refit in 1963, the carriage was used on the Simplon Express and other routes before being withdrawn in 1977. It was bought by Thomas Cook in 1978 to celebrate the company's 50-year association with Wagons-Lits, and was presented on long-term loan to the Nene Valley Railway.

CAR No. 3916

This YT class sleeping car of 1949 is currently in very poor condition, and languishing in a siding.

THE VENICE-SIMPLON-ORIENT EXPRESS

The service had its origins in the Monte Carlo sale of old Wagons-Lits carriages, two of which were purchased by James B. Sherwood, with a view to restoring the glories of the Orient Express. On 25 May 1982, passengers again gathered for the train for Venice. They began their journey in traditional brown and cream Pullman coaches, but once over the Channel they were transferred to the famous royal blue of Wagons-Lits. Further services were added, and to celebrate the millennium a through train ran once more from Paris to Istanbul.

CAR No. 3309

Built by Les Ateliers de Construction Métallurgique in Belgium in 1926, this is one of the first all-steel S class coaches. A notable feature of this carriage is the Art Deco marquetry designed by

René Prou, with highly stylised plant motifs. The car was used on various Orient Express routes from 1929 to 1939, and was involved in the famous freezing winter of that first year. Fortunately for the passengers, it was not left stranded in the wilderness, but came to a halt at the station of Alpullu in the Turkish mountains. The carriage later worked in Germany from 1942 to 1945. after which it was tracked down by Wagons-Lits and put back on the Orient Express. In 1958, it was sent to Portugal, and the interior was modified to take 24 passengers instead of the original 16. It was withdrawn from service in 1971.

CAR No. 3425

Also with designs by Prou, this car was built by the Birmingham Railway Carriage and Wagon Company in 1929. Shipped out on the continental train ferry from Harwich to Zeebrugge, it had a varied career on the Orient Express network and on the Engadine Oberland Express, connecting Paris to the fashionable ski resort of St Moritz. At the outbreak of war, the car was back on the Simplon-Orient Express and was one of the carriages attached to the train in which King Carol of Romania and Magda Lupescu fled to exile. In 1940, the car was sent to Turkey, and ended the first stage of its working life in Portugal.

CAR No. 3473

Built by Metropolitan Cammell in Birmingham, this car has marquetry by the English designer Morison, in a conventional 'flower garland' pattern, with bunches of flowers contained in a border of stylised swags. The carriage ran on the Blue Train until 1937, when it joined the Nord Express, running from Paris to the Russian border. It remained in Paris during the war, and was restored to the Blue Train in 1946. After being transferred to the Simplon in 1961, it was taken out of service in 1971.

CAR No. 3482

This car, like No. 3473, was built by Metropolitan Cammell, but differs in that the marquetry was designed by Maple and executed by Albert Dunn, whose son was responsible for its restoration. The 'Trapeze' design shows a strong Cubist influence and fits well with the Art Deco look of features such as the metal luggage racks. The car ran on the Blue Train and the Nord Express. During the war years it served as a temporary hotel in Lyon. After the war, it ran on the Blue Train and the Lombardy and Simplon Expresses. It also ran in Spain from 1969 to 1971.

Car No. 3483

As with No. 3473, marquetry is by Morison, this time depicting flowers in baskets. After serving in pre-war years on the Blue Train and the Rome and Nord Expresses, the car was sent to Germany and took a great deal of tracking down before it was rescued in 1946. From 1948, it ran on the Simplon Express, then went to Spain in 1973 for a four-year stint on the Costa Brava Express.

Car Nos 3525, 3539, 3543 and 3544

These cars were all built in France by Entreprises Industrielles Charentaises Aytré, and contain some of René Prou's finest decorative work for Wagons-Lits. The coach design was Sapelli Pearl, and used plaster of Paris inlays to give the pearl-like effect. There are suggestions of flowers, fields and trees, but the overall look is almost abstract. Between them the cars covered a range of routes, mainly on the Orient Express and Blue Train, but also including the Rome Express and service in Spain. Car No. 3525 began its working life on the Pyrénées–Côte d'Argent Express to Biarritz. Car No. 3539 suffered from the decline in demand during the Depression years, and was laid up from 1932 to 1936, re-emerging to work on the Rome Express before another hiatus during the war. In 1945, it was commandeered for use by the US Army Transportation Corps. Car No. 3543 was one of the cars bought at the Monte Carlo auction in 1977. Car No. 3544 enjoyed a dramatic change of fortune. During the war years this handsome vehicle was ignominiously reduced to serving as a brothel at Limoges. As a total contrast, after the war it was sent to Holland to form part of the Royal Train.

Car Nos 3552, 3553 and 3555

The construction of these French-made cars is more or less the same as the previous four, but the decoration is the work of Nelson, instead of Prou. Like the English carriages, they have traditional floral motifs, in this case tiger lilies, carried out in marquetry. Nelson carried the style through to the luggage racks, which look distinctly old-fashioned compared with the other coaches. The restaurant cars have a rather different history from the sleepers, in that Lord Dalziel, having control of both Wagons-Lits and the British Pullman Car Company, placed orders for cars that could be used either in Britain or on the Continent. Many found a role on the Golden Arrow/Flèche d'Or services connecting British passengers to the Orient Express.

Car No. 4095

Built in 1927 by the Birmingham Railway Carriage and Wagon Company for use on the Etoile du Nord (Paris–Amsterdam), this car had places for up to 38 diners. It was later used on the Amsterdam–Lucerne run and the London–Vichy Pullman. It was assigned to the Flèche d'Or in 1932, and finished up in Portugal. In its present form, this carriage is something of a hybrid. Its original marquetry panels were removed during restoration and replaced by lacquer panels from a French-built dining car. These are curious designs that have something of Chinese art, a touch of the naive and more than a hint of Raoul Dufy – but unmistakably date from the 1920s.

Car No. 4110

Built by the same company as No. 4095, this car retains its original British marquetry. The designer is unknown, but the style is very similar to that of Morison, with baskets of flowers and garlands. In the 1930s, the carriage was moved east to work on the Danube Pullman, the Carpathian Express and the King Carol I Pullman. It was taken to Portugal in 1949 and modified to take 41 instead of 38 passengers.

Car No. 4141

This car was made in 1929 at Entreprises Industrielles Charentaises Aytré for the Côte d'Azur Pullman service. The Pullmans built for northern Europe had rather restrained decoration, but this car breathes the spirit of Mediterranean sunshine. The designer René Lalique chose opaque glass as his medium, and Bacchanalian piping fauns and naked nymphs as his theme. But, although the theme is classical, the treatment is wholly modern, and the young ladies with their bobbed hair could have doubled as daring sunbathers. After a varied pre-war career, this beautiful carriage ended service on the Flèche d'Or.

THE PULLMAN-ORIENT EXPRESS

During the 1980s Wagons-Lits, recognising the importance of its role in railway history, restored a number of its old coaches at the company's workshops in Belgium and Italy. The result was the creation of a special train, the Pullman-Orient Express. With a current total of nine carriages, it is used for private or corporate charters and promotional excursions. The Pullman-Orient Express and the Venice-Simplon-Orient Express are the last luxury trains comprising genuine Wagons-Lits coaches still in operation in Europe. In 1991, several of the refurbished Pullman-Orient Express cars, originally dating from the 1920s, were classed by the French Ministry of Culture as Historic Monuments.

Car No. 2869

The dining car *Anatolie* was built in Birmingham in 1925. Its mahogany panelling includes marquetry by Albert Dunn, with typical flower garland motifs. The Pullman table lamps, wall lamps and luggage racks are resplendent in polished bronze. The carriage spent its early years on the grand routes – the Simplon-Orient, the Ostend-Vienna-Orient and the Riviera Express. Until 1985 it worked in Italy, largely on the Rome Express.

CARS NOS 2973, 2976 AND 2979

These three dining cars – in numerical order *Edelweiss*, *Taurus* and *Riviera* – were all built at the Reggio-Emilia workshops in Italy. As with No. 2869, they feature mahogany panels and bronze fittings. Each has seven four-seater tables and seven two-seaters. Between them they saw service on all the various Orient Express trains in pre-war years, and were later used on the Rome Express and other Italian lines until 1963.

CAR NO. 4013

Here is an interesting example of how an ordinary coach could be radically transformed late in its career. Built in Birmingham in 1926, No. 4013 ended the first part of its working life in 1966 as a dining car, after which it was converted into a very luxurious service car. There are two service compartments, seven showers, a laundry room, waiting room and toilets.

CAR NO. 4148

This carriage enjoyed a rather more glamorous rebirth than No. 4013. It was built in Aytré, France, in 1929 as a salon car with a typical Art Deco interior designed by the great René Prou. In its early days, it worked on the Flèche d'Or, the Blue Bird (Paris–Brussels–Amsterdam), the Etoile du Nord and the Sud Express (Paris–Lisbon–Madrid). In 1975, while based in Italy, the carriage was converted into the bar car *Côte d'Azur*, with tables and chairs that could be removed so that passengers could, if they felt the urge, dance their way to Istanbul.

CAR NO. 4151

This Pullman salon, named *Etoile du Nord*, was built at Aytré in 1929. Like No. 4148, it has designs by Prou, in this case with pale birch panelling and pewter inlay in a tulip motif. Until 1939 the car ran on the Côte d'Azur Express. After the war, it served on the Sud and Mistral (Paris–Nice) Expresses, and ended up in 1986 on the Istanbul train, after which it was taken away for restoration.

CAR NO. 4159

Very similar to No. 4151, this salon car was built at the same time, also at Aytré. The difference is in the decor, this time by René Lalique, who used his favourite medium of opaque glass and his preferred subject, voluptuous naiads. The Art Deco lamps, however, are by Prou. Like the other coaches, No. 4159 enjoyed a varied career on the grand express trains, including the Paris–Bordeaux service. In spite of being named *Flèche d'Or*, this seems to be the one route that the car did not grace.

CAR NO. 4160

The most exotic of the carriages, this was another of the Aytré coaches of 1929, again with decoration by Lalique and fittings by Prou. It worked on the Côte d'Azur Express in the pre-war years, and returned to service in 1945 on a variety of routes. In 1951, it was converted into a bar car to serve on the very fashionable Blue Train (Paris–Nice–Ventimiglia–San Remo), and has been used in the making of a number of feature films. The *Train Bleu* car is preserved in its original blue and white livery.

ABOVE *The fine craftsmanship found on the Orient Express can be seen in these René Lalique-designed glass panels.*

ABOVE *Car No. 4141 was a Pullman car that in later years worked on the Flèche d'Or. The Lalique panels feature Bacchanalian maidens.*

ABOVE *This British-built S class coach compartment features a sofa bed and flower garland marquetry by Morison.*

Chronology

1845
Georges Nagelmackers born in Liège, Belgium.

1865
George Pullman's coach *Pioneer* is used to carry President Abraham Lincoln's body from Washington to Illinois.

1869
Nagelmackers visits America and travels in Pullman coaches.

1870
Nagelmackers et Cie is formed to promote the use of 'Wagons-Lits' in Europe.

1872
Nagelmackers orders the first five sleeping cars, and founds Compagnie Internationale des Wagons-Lits.

1873
Nagelmackers forms a partnership with Colonel William Mann to run sleeping cars based on the Mann Boudoir Car.

George Pullman reaches agreement with the Midland Railway in Britain to operate his luxury cars. The first Pullman cars go into production at Derby.

1876
Nagelmackers buys out Mann and the Compagnie Internationale is re-formed.

1882
Wagons-Lits runs its first restaurant car between Marseilles and Nice.

The first complete train of Wagons-Lits coaches, including sleeping cars and restaurant car, runs from Paris to Vienna.

1883
The first run of the Orient Express between Paris and Constantinople.

1887
A special set of coaches is built for the president of France.

1889
A complete through route by train is established for the Orient Express from Paris to Constantinople.

1891
The Express d'Orient is officially renamed the Orient Express.

1893
Davison Dalziel of the British Pullman Car Company becomes director of Wagons-Lits.

1894
A second Orient Express route is opened to the steamer port of Constanta on the Black Sea.

1898
A celebratory dinner is organised to mark the 25th anniversary of Wagons-Lits.

1905
The death of Nagelmackers; Dalziel takes control.

1906
Completion of the Simplon tunnel and inauguration of the Simplon Express from Paris to Milan. Work begins on Milan Central Station.

1907
The Simplon Express is extended to Venice.

1912
The Simplon Express is extended to Trieste.

Routes from London to Calais are included as part of the Orient Express timetable.

1913
The South Eastern and Chatham Railway begins a through service from London to Paris.

1914
The outbreak of war brings Wagons-Lits services to an end.

1916
Germany appropriates Wagons-Lits rolling stock in eastern Europe to form Mitropa and inaugurates their own version of the Orient Express – der Balkan Zug.

1918

Marshal Foch accepts the German surrender in Wagons-Lits car No. 2419.

1919

The Train de Luxe Militaire is run for army personnel from Paris to Prague and Bucharest.

A new route is established for the Simplon-Orient Express, with links to Constanta and Athens. It also has connections with trains from London and with the Bordeaux–Milan Express.

1922

The first metal coaches are built and are painted in royal blue.

The Calais Méditerranée Express becomes the Blue Train.

1924

An express service exclusively made up of Pullman cars is run from London to Dover.

1926

The inauguration of the Flèche d'Or service from Calais to Paris using Pullman coaches.

1928

Wagons-Lits acquires the British travel agents Thomas Cook.

Death of Dalziel.

1929

The Golden Arrow Company goes into service from London to Dover, using identical Pullman coaches to those of the Flèche d'Or. The company uses its own ferry, *Canterbury*.

1930

The Simplon-Orient Express is extended to Aleppo as the Taurus Express.

1931

A saboteur blows up the Biatobargy viaduct while the Orient Express is crossing it.

1932

Second-class compartments are introduced on the Flèche d'Or.

1936

The first night ferry service is inaugurated, carrying sleeping cars across the English Channel.

1938

Germany annexes Austria, and Mitropa takes over Wagons-Lits services in both Austria and Czechoslovakia.

1939

Start of World War II and all Orient Express services are suspended.

1940

Germany accepts the French surrender in car No. 2419, which is later taken to Berlin and destroyed.

Mitropa takes over Wagons-Lits rolling stock in eastern Europe, which is widely dispersed.

1945

The end of World War II. Cross-channel ferries resume operations. An invited party join a special run of the Arlberg Express.

1946

The Simplon-Orient Express, and Golden Arrow and Flèche d'Or services are reinstated.

1947

The night ferry is reinstated. Wagons-Lits services are withdrawn in Yugoslavia.

The Balt-Orient Express is inaugurated, linking Scandinavia to the Baltic states.

1948

The Orient Express runs through Czechoslovakia, but services are stopped in Romania.

1949

Hungary is closed to all Wagons-Lits services.

1950

Wagons-Lits leaves Bulgaria and Czechoslovakia.

1952

The Orient Express is rerouted through Yugoslavia and Greece to Istanbul.

1953

The Tauern-Orient Express makes its first run from Ostend to Athens.

1955

The Balkan Express is inaugurated to link the Orient Express at Vienna to Belgrade and Athens.

1961

Wagons-Lits announces that it is to end the running of the direct Orient Express.

1969

The direct Orient Express runs again.

1972

The last run of the Golden Arrow.

1977

The last run of the Orient Express.

Old Wagons-Lits sleeping and restaurant cars are auctioned at Monte Carlo.

1982

A new service using vintage Wagons-Lits sleeping and Pullman cars goes into operation from London to Venice as the Venice-Simplon-Orient Express.

1988

Wagons-Lits launches the Pullman-Orient Express, a special train comprising refurbished carriages and used primarily for private or corporate charters.

Bibliography

NON-FICTION

Barsley, Michael, *Orient Express*, McDonald, 1966

Behrend, George, *Pullman in Europe*, Ian Allen, 1962
   Grand European Expresses, George Allen and Unwin, 1962
   History of Trains de Luxe, Transport Publishing Company, 1977

Behrend, George and Buchanan, Gary, *Night Ferry*, Jersey Artists Ltd., 1985

Cars, Jean des and Caracalla, Jean-Paul, *The Orient Express*, Juillard, 1988

Collett, Emmanuel (ed), *Le Voyage à Constantinople, L'Orient-Express*, Snoeck-Ducaju & Zoon-Pandora, 1988

Commault, Roger, *Georges Nagelmackers*, Editions de la Capitelle, 1972

Cookridge, E.H. *Orient Express*, Allen Lane, 1978

Franzke, Jürgen (ed.), *The Orient Express – Monarch of the Rails*, D.B. Museum Nuremberg, 1998

Hasenson, A., *The Golden Arrow*, Howard Baker, 1970

Hogg, Gary, *The Orient Express*, Hutchinson, 1968

Morel, Julian, *Pullman*, David & Charles, 1983

Sherwood, Shirley, *Venice-Simplon Orient Express*, Weidenfeld & Nicolson, 1983

Wiesenthal, M., *The Belle Epoque of the Orient Express*, Geocolor SA, 1979

FICTION

Ambler, Eric, *The Mask of Dimetrios*, Hodder & Stoughton, 1939

Christie, Agatha, *Murder on the Orient Express*, Collins, 1934

Dekobra, Maurice, *La Madone des Sleepings*, Beaudiniere, 1925
   translation, *The Madonna of Sleeping Cars*, Paul Elek, 1959

Doolard, Den A., *Express to the East*, Arthur Barker, 1936

Fleming, Ian, *From Russia with Love*, Jonathan Cape, 1957

Greene, Graham, *Stamboul Train*, Heinemann, 1932

Roberts, Cecil, *Victoria, Four-Thirty*, Hodder & Stoughton, 1937

White, Ethel Lina, *The Wheel Spins*, Collins, 1936

Index

PICTURE CREDITS

All photographs and illustrations supplied by **Compagnie Internationale des Wagons-Lits (CIWL), Paris, all rights reserved Wagons-Lits Diffusion 2000** except the following:
Anthony Burton: 44, 45
Hulton Getty: 63
Photothèque La Vie du Rail, Paris: 18–19, 26–27, 28–29, 52 (t), 55 (b), 62, 77 (br), 81
Deutsches Museum, Munich: Endpapers

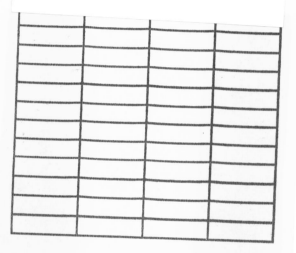

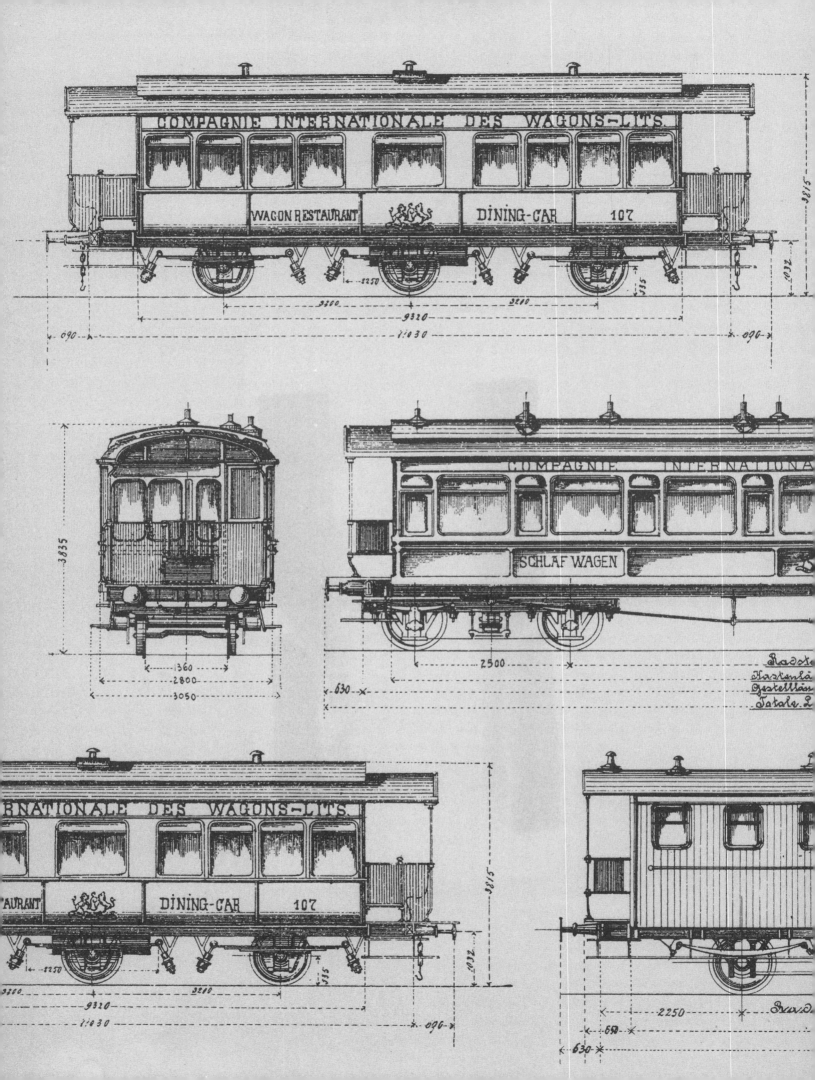